PJ Gray
Stanley Hunter

Bear Cookin'
The Original Guide
to Bear Comfort Foods

Pre-publication
REVIEWS,
COMMENTARIES,
EVALUATIONS . . .

"**L**ike most Bear types, I love food. I especially love the joy and comfort I receive from cooking and the satisfaction of providing others with a 'good' home-cooked meal. It is a very personal experience for me, a method of showing affection, appreciation, and a gift of sorts.

This is what Gray and Hunter have provided with *Bear Cookin'*. It is their personal homage to American home cooking and its deep-rooted influence on your comfort food psyche. Each delicious recipe entices you to try their rich, savory, mouthwatering offerings. This book also proves that an easy and quick recipe does not sacrifice flavor or size in portion, if that is your liking. *Bear Cookin'* is a must for almost any recipe and truly has the makings of a sequel. This is a collector's cookbook."

Dan Stull
Past President,
Great Lakes Bears Chicago

"**G**ray and Hunter have gathered many of their tried and true favorite recipes, creating a culinary tour of stick-to-your-ribs regional American cooking and popular ethnic dishes. From Peach Canyon Quesadillas to Sausage Gravy and Biscuits, or Green Bean Casserole to Grandma's Homemade Ice Cream, there are comfort food recipes for every palate.

Gray and Hunter are serious devotees to home cooking. Gray was raised on Southern cooking and Hunter comes from a long line of restaurateurs. This is a practical cookbook, from snacks to breakfast, lunch, and dinner—entrées, side dishes, and one-dish meals—and culminating with desserts (for those who still have room). They provide tongue-in-cheek tributes to basic Bear food groups, such as Velveeta, microwave popcorn, and cream of mushroom soup. Best of all, they make it okay to eat Cool Whip right out of the tub!"

Les Wright
Editor, *The Bear Book*
and *The Bear Book II;*
Founder, The Bear History Project

More pre-publication
REVIEWS, COMMENTARIES, EVALUATIONS . . .

"This is an outstanding cookbook! Readers will enjoy using it to entertain. The recipes are full of crazy fun and innovative ways of making comfort foods. This book will definitely make all Bears crave comfort food every day, and make a great addition to anyone's cookbook collection."

Patrick Wiese
Executive Sous-Chef,
Carlyn Berghoff Catering,
Chicago

"Hold on to your fork and knife because this cookbook is pure indulgence! *Bear Cookin'* takes a delicious and playful look at hearty home-style comfort foods. Bears, or anyone with a Bearish appetite, will love to try these easy, flavorful recipes! It's like a big, heaping slice of Americana smothered in gravy!"

Mark Donoway
Chef; Author,
The Cucina Bella Cookbook

Harrington Park Press®
An Imprint of The Haworth Press, Inc.
New York • London • Oxford

Bear Cookin'
The Original Guide to Bear Comfort Foods

HARRINGTON PARK PRESS
Titles of Related Interest

The Bear Book: Readings in the History and Evolution of a Gay Male Subculture edited by Les Wright

The Bear Book II: Further Readings in the History and Evolution of a Gay Male Subculture edited by Les Wright

The Bear Handbook: A Comprehensive Guide for Those Who Are Husky, Hairy, and Homosexual and Those Who Love 'Em by Ray Kampf

Bear Like Me by Jonathan Cohen

Bear Cookin'
The Original Guide to Bear Comfort Foods

PJ Gray
Stanley Hunter

Harrington Park Press®
An Imprint of The Haworth Press, Inc.
New York • London • Oxford

Published by

Harrington Park Press®, an imprint of The Haworth Press, Inc., 10 Alice Street, Binghamton, NY 13904-1580.

TR: 10.27.03

Cover design by Marylouise E. Doyle.

Illustrated by Kristin Hanson.

Library of Congress Cataloging-in-Publication Data

Gray, PJ
    Bear cookin' : the original guide to bear comfort foods / PJ Gray, Stanley Hunter.
      p. cm.
    ISBN 1-56023-425-3 — ISBN 1-56023-426-1
    1. Cookery. I. Hunter, Stanley. II. Title.

TX714 .G7429 2003
641.5—dc21

                         2002011968

To all who find comfort in food

ABOUT THE AUTHORS

PJ Gray, a native Floridian, is an award-winning freelance writer and a proud member of the Bear community. He is a featured writer for *Pride* magazine and a contributor to *Rebel Yell 2: More Stories of Contemporary Southern Gay Men* (Harrington Park Press). He currently lives in Chicago.

Stanley Hunter hails from the Chicago area and comes from a family of restaurateurs—as his passion for food, extensive recipe collection, and Bearish frame attest. He is a trend consultant/merchandiser for a globally recognized Chicago-based retailer.

CONTENTS

Foreword   xi
　　　　　Ray Kampf

Acknowledgments   xiii

Introduction   1

SECTION I: LIP SMACKIN' SNACKIN'

Sweet Kibble   5
Raunchy Ranch Munch   6
Onion Ring Beer Batter   7
Auntie's Dill Dip   8
Cheese on Rye Pizzas   9
Microwave Popcorn   10
Mini Franks   11
Bear Belly Bombers   12
Pizza Burgers   13
Big Banana Shake   14
Chili-and-Chip Dip   15
Cookie Brittle   16
Fruity Barbecue Wings   17
Peach Canyon Quesadillas   18

SECTION II: WOOFY BREAKFAST

Hobo Hash   21
Dutch Apple Pancakes   22
Woofy Breakfast Stew   24
Sausage Gravy and Biscuits   25
No Bear Kitchen Is Complete Without . . . Bisquick   26
Bear-to-Go Sandwich   27
Popovers   28
Corn Potato Frittata   29
Real Bears Eat Quiche   30
Apple-Nut Cinnamon Rolls   31
(Touch My) Monkey Bread   32

Overnight Rolls   33
Blueberry Orange Muffins   34
Banana Bread   35

SECTION III: HEARTY SIDES

Yankee Potato Salad   39
Deep South Potato Salad   40
Hot German Potato Salad   41
Sweety Potatoes Anna   42
Potato and Onion Casserole   43
Pork Stuffing   44
Cornmeal Dressin'   45
Bear Daddy's Baked Beans   46
No Bear Kitchen Is Complete Without . . . Velveeta 47
Green Bean Casserole   48
Sesame Green Beans   50
Corn Fritters   51
No Bear Kitchen Is Complete Without . . . Cornflakes 52
Easy Cheesy Potato Bake   53
Cabin Fever Soup   54
What's It All About . . . Alfredo   55
Potatoes Chantal   57
Manly, Yes—Macaroni Salad   58

SECTION IV: COME-AND-GET-IT ENTRÉES

Cheesy Chicken Casserole   61
Johnny Bear-Zetti   62
Spaghetti Carbonara   63
(Squeal Like a) Piggy Mac   64
Creole Beans and Sausage   66
Beef Stroganoff   67
Garlic Chicken Stroganoff   68
Fiery Chicken Enchiladas   69
No Bear Kitchen Is Complete Without . . .
    Cream of Mushroom Soup   70
Tuna Rice Skillet   71
Sweet Hot Chili   72
Polar Bear Chili   73

Chinese Chicken Salad   74
Curry Chicken Salad   75
Cub Salad   76
Sweet Pepper Salad   77
What-a-Crock-Pot Stew   78
Brat Bake   79

SECTION V: BEAR MEAT

Husbear Burgers   83
Grandma's Barbecue Beef   84
Fur-ocious Pot Roast   85
Flamin' Flank Steak   86
Uncle Beau's Standing Rib (Big Meat)   88
Beef or Chicken Fajitas   89
Mom's Meat Loaf   90
No Bear Kitchen Is Complete Without . . . Ground Beef   91
Pork Steaks   92
Slow-Simmered Country Ribs   93
Dinner Party Pork Chops   94
Russian River Oven-Baked Fish   95
Grilled Chicken in Lime Curry Sauce   96
Uncle Beau's Sunday Roast Chicken   97

SECTION VI: BEYOND THE HONEYPOT

Very Berry Ruby Cobbler   101
Easy Peach Blueberry Cobbler   102
Lonestar Brownies   103
Banana Pudding   104
Bear in the Woods   105
Cream Puffs   106
Chocolate Loaf   107
No Bear Kitchen Is Complete Without . . . Cool Whip   108
Carrot Zucchini Cake   109
Mom's Oatmeal Pie   110
Nannie's Pecan Pie   111
Daddy's Favorite Peach Pie   113
Banana Split Cake   114
Over-the-Top Easy Bake   115

Our Favorite New York-Style Cheesecake 116
Easy Blueberry Cheesecake 117
Chocolate Pudding Cake 118
Grandma's Homemade Ice Cream 119

Recipe Index **121**

Subject Index **123**

Foreword

When I bought my house a few years ago, the first thing I remodeled was the kitchen—not because I *couldn't* cook surrounded by hideous daisy wallpaper, or on the rather dangerous-looking electric stove the previous owner had left behind; it was because I didn't *want* to cook in a kitchen that was ugly, or on something that could burst into flames while I was whipping up my crème brûlée. For me, cooking is a joyous activity, and the proper setting and equipment makes it all the more enjoyable. Kind of like sex.

You know a Bear is writing this, because although I was asked to write about food and cooking, the subject naturally led to sex. And why shouldn't it all combine? Both are visceral pleasures that should be done with passion. Each bite and nibble should cause your mouth to salivate. Each texture on your tongue should spark a taste bud to tingle. The aroma should fill your nose with a heady scent. Every moment should be savored, whether it's dining or playing. Unfortunately, this is not always the case.

Bear meals are too frequently reduced to a drive-thru burger, or the quick consumption of a Jenny Craig prepackaged morsel. Food shouldn't always be easy. Sometimes the effort of creating a meal pays off better than you could ever expect. A hearty dinner made with love often yields better results than an expert tongue. That is where the beauty of this book comes in handy.

Although most Bears can muddle their way around the kitchen, some Bears don't know a lot about food. Some believe that food comes in a cardboard box and is delivered by a scrawny kid in a Domino's Pizza hat. Food has to come from *somewhere*. It comes from an act (or an art) called "cooking." Cooking is taking ingredients (raw foods), putting them together in various proportions, and heating them in certain ways to create what is called a "prepared dish." You may have seen something like this at a restaurant when the server brings a plate to the table. Or you may have witnessed this act of cooking on television shows such as *Martha Stewart Living, Emeril*

Live, or *Iron Chef.* These chefs are professionals and may intimidate you, but don't be afraid. Cooking is for everyone—in particular, for Bears!

When I was but a young cub and attending my first Bear event, a pool party, everyone was instructed to bring a covered dish. (I think I brought a carved-out rye bread with a spinach dip.) The orgy of food that was heaped upon the picnic table was accompanied by comments such as "Who made this? It's delicious" and "I need the recipe for that!" There was also the snide "He only opened a can of baked beans!" whispered about one of the party guests. These big butch men were all of a sudden my mother's card club commenting on how good (or how ill prepared) each dish was. It didn't just happen there; wherever Bears gathered, food was discussed.

PJ and Stanley have brought together a collection of recipes that can satisfy any Bear appetite, not just because the dishes taste good in the end, but because it gives us a chance to create and get messy in the kitchen. Some recipes are simple and quick. Some recipes are much more complex. These are the ones that fill your nostrils with delightful smells. These are the ones you prepare for a dinner party to linger over with friends. These are the ones you make for a special someone. But all of the recipes, simple or complex, are designed to make cooking an enjoyable experience.

Ray Kampf
Author, The Bear Handbook

Acknowledgments

We would like to thank our families not only for their love and support but also for their talent and inspiration. Thank you for a lifetime of comfort food.

We would also like to thank the following friends for their support and/or contribution: John and Stacy Arambages, Claudia Bianchi, Loren Boothby, David Cohen, Lisa Colpoys, Mark Donoway, Janet Hood, Bill Keefe, Kathleen Luster, Tim Lynch, Suzanna McCall, Janet McCleary, Nancy Michael, Margaret Resce Milkint, Beau Nolan, Cindy Riney O'Reilly, Jeff Pietrantoni, Catherine Prete, Jay Quinn, Kathy Schneider, Byron Scott, Katie Scullion, Ann Sherlock, Art Smith, Ron Stoczynski, Debbie Stueckel, Don Stull, Mike Sullivan, Greg Tripp, Natalie Ward, Bill Watters, and Patrick Weise.

Introduction

The idea for this book was sparked at the most appropriate time and place—a dinner between two Bears. This wasn't any ordinary dinner. This was a "hibernation dinner." It was the dead of winter and the food was rich, warm, and delicious. It was just the kind of comfort food we craved during a snowy, frozen evening.

Once our plates were filled, our conversation took a very natural direction. What began as a discussion about favorite foods led to a memorable journey back to our childhoods. We laughed and ate as we shared recollections of holiday meals, compared our mothers' cooking styles, and described favorite recipes. By the end of the meal, we were amazed at how many comfort foods we could name. We also agreed on one simple truth: food is love. It's that simple. Whether it is created from parental love, a friendship, a marriage, or even a love for oneself, food is our communion and it is what makes life worth living.

We also clearly recognized the correlation between most Bears and comfort food. Let's face it. Bears have big appetites and hearty, home-style cooking seems to be the only food that satisfies us. With this in mind, we searched for recipes that were not only hearty but were also flavorful and fairly simple to create. We discovered that the majority of our personal and family recipes seemed to meet these requirements.

Whether you're a Bear or a Bear admirer, we hope that you enjoy this collection of recipes. They are foods that we love, and we're delighted to share them with you. Woof!

SECTION I:
LIP SMACKIN' SNACKIN'

SWEET KIBBLE

Stanley fondly remembers, "My grandmother used to make this, along with our favorite cookies, for the holidays. It was so well liked that she had to make double batches! Now I eat it year-round."

1 pound almond bark
1 (8-ounce) package of peanuts
2 cups pretzels, broken
2 cups crisped rice cereal
1 1/2 cups Cap'n Crunch's Peanut Butter cereal

Melt almond bark in large Crock-Pot. Once completely melted, add all other ingredients and mix until all ingredients are well coated.

Spoon onto waxed paper in tablespoon portions and allow to cool.

Use Your Tool: Crock-Pots are no crock! If you don't already have one, now is the time to own one. They're handy to have around the kitchen for more than Sweet Kibble.

Bearable Meal Suggestions: Beer.

RAUNCHY RANCH MUNCH

This is something worth keeping in a jar on your kitchen counter year-round. "Originally, I was given a variation of this recipe from a Junior Leaguer in Mobile, Alabama, so you know it's good stuff," PJ admits. "I've yet to find a store-bought snack mix that I prefer more than this."

1 package ranch dressing mix
1 tablespoon dried dill weed
1 1/2 teaspoons garlic salt
1 1/2 cups oil (vegetable or canola)
2 (11-ounce) packages oyster crackers

    Mix all ingredients in large covered plastic container or resealable plastic bag and let stand for several hours or overnight.
    Before serving, shake container well. Pour into serving bowl and attack!

Bearable Meal Suggestions: Beer.

ONION RING BEER BATTER

One of the all-time classic beer recipes. Your friends will be so impressed that you can do more with beer than just drink it! Stanley likes to serve these onion rings during summer barbecues.

1 cup sifted all-purpose flour
1/2 teaspoon salt
2 dashes of pepper
1 teaspoon paprika
2 egg yolks
2 egg whites
2/3 cup beer
2 tablespoons melted butter
2 large Vidalia onions
Vegetable oil for deep-frying

Mix all ingredients together except the egg whites and onions, and let stand at room temperature for 90 minutes. Beat egg whites until stiff and fold into existing batter.

Peel and slice onions in half, then pull rings apart. Place rings in batter and coat thoroughly.

Heat oil to 375°F and carefully drop coated onions into the hot oil, in batches. Cook until deep golden brown. Remove and drain on paper towels.

Use Your Tool: As with any cooking occasion that requires hot oil, safety must always be considered. Expect some splattering; an apron is definitely recommended.

Bearable Meal Suggestions: Beer and . . . To spice things up, add a couple of dashes of cayenne pepper to the batter. This gives it a nice fire!

AUNTIE'S DILL DIP

Another of Stanley's holiday favorites. . . . Of course, this should be enjoyed any time of the year. "My aunt used to drive miles out of her way to buy sisal bread from a specific bakery, and it was worth it—it's delicious!"

1 loaf round sisal bread*
1 (16-ounce) container sour cream
1 cup mayonnaise
2 tablespoons dried dill weed
1 tablespoon dried onion flakes
garlic salt to taste

Cut out and hollow center of sisal bread. Tear hollowed-out bread into bite-sized pieces and set aside.

In large mixing bowl, combine all other ingredients and mix well. Pour dip into hollowed center of bread. Place bread on center of platter and surround with bread pieces. Also add cut vegetables for dipping, if desired.

Bearable Meal Suggestions: Beer.

---

*Sisal bread can be found at most Jewish bakeries/delicatessens.

CHEESE ON RYE PIZZAS

"I've always referred to this as a 'crack snack' because it's so addictive," PJ admits. "I once had a friend who went to the store to buy more ingredients immediately after sampling the first batch . . . he was hooked and has been a 'crack snack' junkie ever since."

1 pound pork sausage
4 ounces shredded mozzarella cheese
1 teaspoon garlic salt
3 tablespoons catsup
1/2 pound Velveeta
1 teaspoon dried oregano
2 tablespoons Worcestershire sauce
2 loaves party rye bread

In saucepan, brown sausage then drain excess grease. Add all other ingredients into pan except bread and stir over low heat until cheese is thoroughly melted.

Spread on rye slices and serve. As an option, toast under a broiler or in a toaster oven for a few minutes and serve immediately.

Use Your Tool: Instead of heating up the entire kitchen, this is a great way to benefit from the convenience of a toaster oven.

Bearable Meal Suggestions: Beer.

No Bear Kitchen Is Complete Without . . .

MICROWAVE POPCORN

Grrrrrr. CRUNCH! Grrrrrr. CRUNCH! Grrrrrr. CRUNCH! That's the sound of a Bear devouring one of his favorite snack foods—a mindless snacking condition commonly known as "autofeed." Evidence of this can be found either in the depths of a Bear's chest hair or his sofa.

Nearly two decades have passed since the introduction of microwave popcorn—the ultimate marriage of convenience between food and technology. Although you can purchase it in a variety of flavors, we recommend creating your own signature seasonings. Try adding parmesan cheese, Italian seasoning, bacon bits, or cinnamon and sugar. Whatever your taste, just go for it! It's a snack that eats like a meal.

MINI FRANKS

They could very well be the hottest (but maybe not the smallest) things you've ever put in your mouth. . . . Speak for yourself, right?

3 (8-ounce) cans of biscuits
1 small jar yellow or favorite mustard
5 dozen cocktail wieners

Preheat oven to 475°F. Cut biscuits into 1/2-inch-strips. Spread each strip lightly with mustard, and wrap around a cocktail wiener. Arrange on cookie sheet (seam side down) and bake for 9 minutes.

Dipping Sauce

3 tablespoons dry mustard
1 cup catsup
1/4 cup pickle relish
1 teaspoon onion powder

Mix ingredients together and refrigerate for 1 hour to blend flavors.

Bearable Meal Suggestions: Beer and . . . Stanley once again recommends adding a couple of dashes of cayenne pepper to the mustard or dipping sauce. He loves this stuff!

BEAR BELLY BOMBERS

Brace yourself for the ultimate Bear party snack! Don't be surprised if some of your guests taste a "fast-food familiarity" when these "slide" down. They're cheesy, they're oniony, and they're sure to satisfy big appetites.

2 pounds ground beef
1 (2-ounce) package dry onion soup mix
1 (10-ounce) can cream of mushroom soup
1/2 large block Velveeta, cubed
4 dozen dinner rolls

Brown ground beef in large stockpot and drain excess grease. Add soup mix and canned soup, and stir until combined. Return to low heat and add cubed portions of cheese to mixture. Stir until melted and well combined.

Spoon onto dinner roll-sized bread (not hamburger buns). Makes about fifty servings, unless you're hosting a Bear party. In that case, you'll be lucky to serve twelve Bears.

Use Your Tool: An 8-quart stockpot is ideal, due to the amount of ingredients.

Bearable Meal Suggestions: Beer (if room allows).

CAUTION—This snack may cause immediate hibernation. Make sure a bed is in the vicinity before serving.

PIZZA BURGERS

A great party-sandwich idea. Of course, for most people this would be considered a meal; for Bears, it's definitely a snack.

2 pounds ground beef
2 (10-ounce) cans cream of mushroom soup
2 (8-ounce) cans pizza sauce
1 (8-ounce) package sliced mozzarella cheese
1 package hamburger buns

Preheat oven to 350°F. On stove top, brown and season ground beef to your liking in large saucepan then pour off excess grease. Add pizza sauce and soup; stir well. Heat through and let simmer for about 2 to 3 minutes. Spoon onto open-faced buns assembled on cookie sheet. Place slices of cheese on each. Bake in oven for approximately 5 minutes or until cheese has melted completely.

Use Your Tool: Another reason to invest in a durable, nonstick cookie sheet for oven use.

Bearable Meal Suggestions: Beer.

BIG BANANA SHAKE

More than an innuendo, it's a rich, delicious way to satisfy your sweet tooth in a hurry. Try experimenting with new ingredients. This recipe allows you to be as creative as you want—so go for it!

1 cup sliced banana
1 cup strawberries
1 pint premium vanilla ice cream
1 cup half-and-half

   Add ingredients to blender and blend to a desired consistency.

Use Your Tool: A blender is mandatory for this recipe, so borrow a neighbor's if you must!

Bearable Meal Suggestions: Beer. (OK, maybe not this time.)

CHILI-AND-CHIP DIP

Attention all chili and cheese freaks! This snack is guaranteed to fill you up. It is best savored during winter hibernation.

3 (15-ounce) cans favorite chili
1 pound Velveeta, cubed
1 tablespoon Worcestershire sauce
garlic salt to taste

   Heat ingredients together (preferably in a Crock-Pot) until cheese melts—it's that simple!
   Served best with corn chips, especially the larger chips that can "scoop" well!

Use Your Tool: This is another Crock-Pot recipe. It's a worthy kitchen appliance addition. Buy one!

Bearable Meal Suggestions: Beer.

COOKIE BRITTLE

Hey! Put down that cookie dough in a tube and listen! Try this once and you'll be hooked. It's ideal baking for those cold winter days or to impress a date.

1 cup margarine
1 1/2 teaspoons vanilla
1 teaspoon salt
1 cup sugar
2 cups flour
1 (6-ounce) bag chocolate chips
1/2 cup pecans or walnuts

Preheat oven to 375°F. Combine margarine, vanilla, and salt. Gradually add sugar, then flour and chocolate chips. Mix well and press evenly into an ungreased cookie sheet. Sprinkle nuts over top and bake for 25 minutes. Let cool completely. Break into pieces and serve.

Use Your Tool: This easy recipe is made easier with a heavy-duty kitchen mixer.

Bearable Meal Suggestions: Beer and . . . Ideal for bedtime snacking with a tall glass of milk. (Of course, we recommend sharing!)

FRUITY BARBECUE WINGS

You'll just keep eating and eating and eating them. "Before any of my friends accept an invitation to one of my barbecues, they ask if these will be served," Stanley admits. PJ adds, "This definitely falls into the 'crack snack' category. I just can't stop myself!"

3/4 cup orange juice
1/4 cup lemon juice
1 cup firmly packed brown sugar
2 cups favorite barbecue sauce
40 frozen chicken wing pieces (found in most supermarket frozen-food sections)
2 large navel oranges, sliced and quartered
2 lemons, sliced and quartered

Preheat oven to 325°F. Combine juices, sugar, and barbecue sauce in saucepan over medium heat for approximately 10 minutes, stirring occasionally, until ingredients blend thoroughly.

If frozen, thaw chicken thoroughly and drain any excess water. Place wings in single layer in roasting pan and cover with fruit slices. Pour sauce mixture over top, cover pan with aluminum foil, and bake for 1 hour. Remove foil and bake until sauce thickens, approximately 30 additional minutes.

Use Your Tool: Best cooked in a roasting pan or shallow ovenproof pan.

Bearable Meal Suggestions: Beer.

PEACH CANYON QUESADILLAS

The inspiration for this recipe is the incredible flavor of peach salsa—
it beats any other flavored salsa hands down! These quesadillas are
especially popular with Southwestern Bears.

1/2 teaspoon chili powder
1/2 teaspoon cumin
2 whole chicken breasts, boned and skinned
4 (10-inch) flour tortillas
1/3 cup shredded Monterey Jack cheese
1/3 cup shredded Jalapeno Jack cheese
1 roasted red bell pepper, seeded and diced
1 jar peach salsa*

Preheat broiler. In a small bowl, combine chili powder and cumin—
mix well. Rub mixture on chicken, and broil chicken until just opaque
throughout. Remove from broiler and dice into 1/2-inch cubes.

In skillet over medium-high heat, place a tortilla and top with
cheeses, red pepper, chicken, and salsa. When cheese melts and tortillas are lightly browned, fold in half and transfer to a cutting board.
Cut each into quarters.

Garnish with guacamole and/or sour cream and additional salsa.
Serve at once.

Use Your Tool: A great way to test out your nonstick frying pan.

Bearable Meal Suggestions: Beer and . . . guacamole or chunky salsa
for garnish.

---

*If peach salsa cannot be found at your local grocer, dice fresh peaches into your
favorite salsa and warm over medium heat to blend flavors.

SECTION II:
WOOFY BREAKFAST

HOBO HASH

"This is another Sunday morning favorite from my childhood," Stanley recalls. "My father used to grill extra baked potatoes on Saturday so he could make this dish the next day."

1 red pepper, finely diced
1 yellow onion, finely diced
1 (16-ounce) tube pork sausage
5 eggs, beaten
3 large potatoes, cooked, cubed, with skin*

In a nonstick skillet, sauté red pepper and onion for approximately 10 minutes on medium heat. Remove from skillet. In same skillet, crumble and cook sausage until browned.

Remove sausage from skillet. In same skillet, sauté potatoes over medium heat until golden brown. Add cooked red pepper, onion, and sausage back into skillet with potatoes.

Pour beaten eggs over all other ingredients and continue cooking over medium heat. Using a spatula, lift hash mixture in sections and turn over to cook eggs thoroughly.

Remove hash from skillet in spatula-sized portions and serve.

Bearable Meal Suggestions: Beer and . . . Serve with Blueberry Orange Muffins (page 34) or Popovers (page 28).

---

*May substitute 1 can sliced white potatoes.

DUTCH APPLE PANCAKES

If a five-star rating system were created for this book, Dutch Apple Pancakes would rate at least ten stars! Stanley fondly remembers, "My grandfather owned a restaurant and served these only on Sunday mornings because demand was so overwhelming." In more recent years, Stanley has impressed many a Bear "the morning after" with this delicious treat. Woof!

1/2 cup whole milk
1/2 cup flour
3 eggs
1 teaspoon sugar
dash of salt
6 tablespoons butter
3 to 4 green apples, peeled and sliced
dash of cinnamon

Preheat oven to 450°F. To prepare pancake batter, thoroughly blend the milk, flour, eggs, sugar, and salt.

In a cast-iron (or ovenproof) skillet, melt 2 tablespoons of butter and add the sliced apples. Fry on stove top until soft. Pour batter over apples and bake in oven for 8 minutes.

When pancake is partially baked, remove from oven and sprinkle with cinnamon, sugar, and dot with 4 tablespoons remaining butter. Return skillet to oven and bake an additional 8 minutes. Serve hot with maple syrup.

Use Your Tool: A 10-inch seasoned cast-iron skillet is ideal. Also, a blender makes mixing the batter much easier.

Bearable Meal Suggestions: Beer and . . . Serve with your favorite link or patty breakfast sausage.

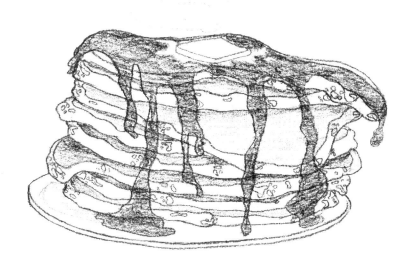

WOOFY BREAKFAST STEW

We know what you're thinking—"Grits?" Trust us, you've never had them like this. But we must warn you: this recipe is for serious breakfast eaters!

10 slices bacon
1 (16-ounce) tube spicy sausage
6 eggs
1 (8-ounce) block extra-sharp cheddar cheese, cubed
3 whole English muffins
1 (24-ounce) container "quick-style" grits
4 tablespoons minced onions
1 (8-ounce) package shredded sharp cheddar cheese
salt and pepper to taste

In a skillet, fry bacon, drain, and remove from skillet. Follow the same steps with the sausage. Scramble and season the eggs and set aside.

While frying the meats, toast the English muffin halves, cut into bite-sized pieces, and set aside.

In a large boiler or stockpot, cook grits using the instructions on box for 18 servings. Add salt, pepper, and minced onion as grits cook down or thicken. Then add cubes of the extra-sharp cheddar cheese and stir until melted. Add final seasoning to grits until desired taste is achieved.

Add remaining ingredients and mix thoroughly. Spoon into cereal bowls and garnish with shredded sharp cheddar cheese.

Use Your Tool: You'll need a skillet for frying, a toaster for toasting, and a large stockpot for cooking the grits.

Bearable Meal Suggestions: Beer and . . . Actually, this is a complete meal in itself and suited for a group breakfast. Fruit juices or coffee may accompany.

SAUSAGE GRAVY AND BISCUITS

Definitely a Saturday or Sunday morning meal—especially suited for "hangover mornings." Enough said.

1 pound bulk pork sausage
2 tablespoons dried onion
6 tablespoons flour
1 quart milk
dash of salt
1/2 teaspoon poultry seasoning
1/2 teaspoon nutmeg
dash of Worcestershire sauce

In a large skillet, cook sausage thoroughly, adding dried onion toward the end of the cooking time. Drain excess grease with the exception of approximately 2 tablespoons. Add flour and cook over medium heat for 6 minutes. Stir in milk gradually, followed by seasonings. Cook until thickened. Pour over ready-made biscuits or try our easy scratch biscuit recipe that follows.

Scratch Biscuits

2 cups all-purpose flour
1 teaspoon baking powder
2 teaspoons sugar
1/2 teaspoon cream of tartar
1/4 teaspoon salt
1/2 cup butter
2/3 cup milk

Preheat oven to 450°F. In a large mixing bowl, use a fork and knife and begin by cutting dry ingredients into butter until coarse crumbs form. Create a "well" in the center of mixture and add milk. Stir until dough clings. Knead the dough approximately 10 to 12 strokes. Roll or pat dough to desired thickness. Let dough rest for approximately 10 to 15 minutes before baking. Cut dough into round biscuit-sized pieces. Bake for 10 to 12 minutes.

Bearable Meal Suggestions: Beer and . . . juice, coffee, aspirin, or, in extreme cases, Bloody Marys.

No Bear Kitchen
Is Complete Without . . .

BISQUICK

Remember hot fluffy biscuits fresh from the oven? Giant waffles served piping hot from your mother's waffle iron? And those pancakes! Thick golden brown pancakes the size of your plate and stacked a mile high, covered in butter and warm maple syrup. Woof!

Chances are very likely that your mother and even your grandmother created these delicious food memories using one of our favorite products—Bisquick, America's premiere convenience baking mix.

This versatile baking invention dates back to 1930 and, thanks to the chemists and executives at General Mills, has contributed greatly to many of our favorite meals. We believe it will continue to stand the test of time as food trends and eating habits continue to evolve. In fact, we encourage you to always keep a box in your kitchen. Try their Impossibly Easy Cheeseburger Pie; it is guaranteed to satisfy any Bear's appetite. If the recipe is not on the side of the box, go to <www.BettyCrocker.com>!

BEAR-TO-GO SANDWICH

Here's another quick and delicious toaster-oven classic for active Bears. "This qualifies as a great snack recipe as well. It became my favorite midnight snack because I couldn't wait until breakfast," PJ confesses.

4 hard-boiled eggs*, chopped
1/4 cup cheddar cheese, shredded
2 1/2 tablespoons French dressing
1 teaspoon real bacon pieces/bits (can be found in can at grocer)
2 to 4 toasted waffles, English muffins, or bread slices
Thin tomato slices, optional

In a medium-sized bowl, stir together eggs, cheese, dressing, and bacon until blended.

Cover and chill to blend flavors.

Spread half of the mixture on each of 2 waffles. In oven or toaster oven, broil 6 inches from heat until warm, about 3 minutes. Garnish with tomato slices, if desired. Top with additional waffles, if desired.

Use Your Tool: A toaster oven is a more convenient option to a standard oven, but not necessary.

Bearable Meal Suggestions: Beer and . . . coffee or juice.

---

*To hard-boil eggs: Place a single layer of eggs in saucepan. Add enough water to come at least one inch above eggs. Cover. Quickly bring to boil and then turn off heat. If necessary, remove pan from burner to prevent further boiling. Let eggs stand, covered, in the hot water (for medium eggs—12 minutes; for large eggs—15 minutes; for extra-large eggs—18 minutes). Immediately run cold water over eggs or place them in ice water until completely cooled. Peel.

POPOVERS

"I love popovers because they're easier to make than they look," PJ admits. "My friends are always impressed; they think I slaved over them. Of course, I'll never tell them the truth."

3 eggs
1 1/4 cups milk, at room temperature
1 tablespoon vegetable oil
1 pinch salt
1 1/4 cups all-purpose flour

Preheat oven to 450°F. Grease popover tin or muffin tin lightly (oil all surfaces). Beat eggs with whisk or hand mixer until lemon-colored and foamy. Add milk; blend well, but do not overbeat. Add salt and flour all at once. Beat until foamy and smooth on top.

Pour popover batter into a pitcher so that it can be easily poured. Fill popover tin with batter. (If using a muffin tin, fill every other cup, so when popovers puff they will not touch one another.) Bake for 15 minutes at 450°F, then turn heat down to 350°F and bake for an additional 30 minutes. DO NOT OPEN OVEN DOOR WHILE BAKING.

When ready to serve, remove popovers from tin with a sharp knife.

Strawberry Butter

1 pound (4 sticks) unsalted butter
3/4 cup strawberry preserves

Soften butter to room temperature. Using an electric mixer, whip in preserves. Cover mixture and refrigerate. Best served at room temperature.

Use Your Tool: Unless you're experienced with a whisk (in the kitchen), a hand mixer is easier.

Bearable Meal Suggestions: Beer and . . . Try them with bacon and eggs.

CORN POTATO FRITTATA

Tired of the monotony of Jethro-sized bowls of cereal morning after morning? Break the habit with this incredible frittata! "I used to be satisfied with just cheese and eggs—not anymore," PJ says.

1 (16-ounce) tube sausage
2 garlic cloves, minced
3 tablespoons olive oil
2 large russet (baking) potatoes, peeled and diced into 1/4-inch
    pieces
2 cups corn kernels (10 ounces), thawed if frozen
4 large eggs
4 ounces mozzarella, coarsely shredded

Cook and crumble sausage, then drain and set aside in separate bowl. Cook garlic in 2 tablespoons oil in a 10-inch nonstick skillet over medium heat for approximately 2 minutes, or until softened. Add potatoes and cook over medium-low heat, stirring until tender, for approximately 10 minutes. Add cooked sausage, corn, and salt and pepper to taste; then cook, stirring for about 1 minute.

Preheat broiler. Whisk together eggs, mozzarella, and salt and pepper to taste. Stir in potato mixture.

Heat remaining tablespoon of oil in a cast-iron skillet over medium heat until hot but not smoking. Then add egg and potato mixture and cook without stirring, shaking skillet once or twice to loosen frittata, until underside is golden but top is still wet (about 6 minutes). Remove from heat.

Broil frittata approximately 3 inches from heat until top is just golden (about 2 minutes).

Remove from oven, slide onto plate, and cool to warm or room temperature.

Bearable Meal Suggestions: Beer and . . . This is the perfect brunch recipe! Serve with any brunch items.

REAL BEARS EAT QUICHE

This recipe is designed to challenge novice cooks. It's still a fairly simple recipe, but requires a little more prep time. The effort and time is definitely worth the wait!

Nonstick cooking spray
1 pound russet potatoes, peeled and sliced into 1/4-inch rounds
garlic powder to taste
1 tablespoon olive oil
1 cup chopped onion
1 cup chopped red bell pepper
1/2 teaspoon dried thyme
1 cup Italian sausage, cooked and chopped
8 large eggs
1/4 teaspoon salt
1/4 teaspoon ground black pepper
1 cup shredded smoked cheddar or Gouda cheese

Preheat oven to 350°F. Coat 10-inch glass pie dish with cooking spray. Steam potato rounds until just tender, about 6 minutes. Transfer to rack and cool. Line the prepared pie dish with enough potato rounds to cover, overlapping slightly. Sprinkle garlic powder over potatoes.

Heat olive oil in large saucepan over medium-high heat. Add onion, red bell pepper, and thyme; sauté 5 minutes. Add Italian sausage and sauté until heated through, about 1 minute. Spoon sausage mixture over potatoes in pie dish.

Whisk eggs, salt, and pepper in a large bowl, then blend in cheese. Pour egg mixture over sausage mixture in pie dish and bake until set in center, about 35 minutes. Cool 20 minutes.

Cut into wedges. Serve warm or at room temperature.

Bearable Meal Suggestions: Beer and . . . This quiche also makes a wonderful dinner entrée when served with tossed salad (heavy dressing, please!) and hot buttered dinner rolls.

APPLE-NUT CINNAMON ROLLS

After making this once, you'll never want to eat refrigerated biscuits the same way again!

1/2 cup heavy cream
2 large tart baking apples
1/2 cup chopped pecans or walnuts
1 cup sugar
1 teaspoon ground cinnamon
2 (10-ounce) cans refrigerated biscuits
1/2 cup butter or margarine, melted

Preheat oven to 350°F. Pour cream into a 13 x 9 x 2-inch baking pan. Peel and chop apples into small pieces. Sprinkle apples and nuts evenly over the cream.

In a shallow bowl, combine sugar and cinnamon. Dip biscuits in melted butter, then into cinnamon-sugar. Arrange biscuits over apple-nut mixture.

Bake, uncovered, for 25 minutes.

Use Your Tool: This recipe reminds us how a baking pan can be an important and versatile kitchen accessory.

Bearable Meal Suggestions: Beer and . . . Great with omelets!

(TOUCH MY) MONKEY BREAD

Bears who love to eat with their hands will love to pull apart this sticky, sweet, caramel-coated bread. Enjoy this any time of the day!

4 (10-ounce) cans refrigerated biscuits
1/2 cup sugar
1 tablespoon cinnamon
1 cup melted butter
1 cup brown sugar
1 cup chopped nuts

Preheat oven to 350°F. Cut each biscuit into quarters. Combine sugar and cinnamon in a bowl. Roll biscuit pieces lightly in your hand to make a round shape. Roll these in sugar-cinnamon mixture. Stack coated pieces evenly into a greased angel food cake pan.

Combine butter, brown sugar, and nuts. Pour evenly over pieces.

Bake for 45 minutes. Allow to cool slightly and invert pan onto plate to remove bread.

Use Your Tool: Angel food cake pans are not the same as bundt cake pans. Avoid using a bundt cake pan for this recipe.

Bearable Meal Suggestions: Beer and . . . Another great bread to serve with bacon and eggs!

OVERNIGHT ROLLS

It's all in the timing . . . and well worth getting out of bed for this mouthwatering breakfast. The quick prep time the night before makes this one of our easiest and most delicious morning recipes in the book—enjoy!

1 dozen frozen dinner rolls
1 (3-ounce) package butterscotch pudding (NOT INSTANT)
3/4 cup brown sugar
1/2 cup margarine, sliced into pats
chopped pecans, if desired

Place frozen dinner rolls in a greased 9 x 13-inch cake pan. Sprinkle dry pudding, brown sugar, margarine, and nuts on top, then cover pan with plastic wrap. Leave covered at room temperature overnight.

In the morning, remove plastic wrap and place pan in oven. DO NOT PREHEAT OVEN.

Bake at 350°F for 20 minutes.

Use Your Tool: A 9 x 13-inch baking pan is a smart addition to any kitchen and ideal for this recipe.

Bearable Meal Suggestions: Beer and . . . These can also be prepped in the morning and baked at night for a late-night snack!

BLUEBERRY ORANGE MUFFINS

Never thought you were much of a baker? Prove yourself wrong with this easy muffin recipe. "When blueberries are in season, I like to bake these often," Stanley confesses. "Now my friends can't wait for blueberry season. I wonder why?"

1 cup quick rolled oats
1 cup orange juice
1 cup vegetable oil
3 eggs, beaten
3 cups all-purpose flour
1 cup sugar
4 teaspoons baking powder
1 teaspoon salt
1/2 teaspoon baking soda
3 to 4 cups fresh blueberries

Topping

1/2 cup finely chopped pecans or walnuts
3 tablespoons sugar
1/2 teaspoon cinnamon

Preheat oven to 400°F. Mix oats and orange juice; blend in oil and eggs and set aside. In another bowl, stir together flour, sugar, baking powder, salt, and baking soda. Add oat mixture and mix lightly. Fold in blueberries. Spoon batter into paper-lined muffin pans, filling 2/3 full. Combine topping ingredients and sprinkle over batter. Bake for approximately 15 to 18 minutes or until lightly browned.

Bearable Meal Suggestions: Beer and . . . Great with Hobo Hash (page 21).

BANANA BREAD

"When we were planning this section, banana bread was one of our top choices," PJ shares. "Growing up, this recipe was not only a great breakfast treat but also present during so many occasions—school and church functions, housewarming parties, and even as Christmas gifts."

1 cup granulated sugar
1/2 cup (1 stick) butter or margarine
2 eggs, beaten
1 1/2 cups mashed bananas (3 or 4)
1 tablespoon lemon juice
2 cups sifted all-purpose flour (sift before measuring)
1 tablespoon baking powder
1/2 teaspoon salt
1 cup chopped pecans or walnuts

Preheat oven to 350°F. Grease a 9 x 5 x 3-inch loaf pan. Beat sugar with butter until light. Add eggs one at a time, beating well after each addition. Stir in bananas and lemon juice.

Sift flour with baking powder and salt; add to banana mixture and stir in quickly. Stir in nuts.

Pour into prepared pan and bake 1 hour.

Use Your Tool: Important tools for this recipe include the correct sized loaf pan and a flour sifter.

Bearable Meal Suggestions: Beer and . . . hot chocolate or coffee.

SECTION III:
HEARTY SIDES

YANKEE POTATO SALAD

Stanley explains, "I grew up in the upper Midwest, and PJ is from the South. We both remember our families making potato salad but in very different ways. So we thought it would be interesting to share both versions. Here's mine . . . "

3 pounds red potatoes
1/3 cup dry white wine
1 small red bell pepper, seeded and diced

Vinaigrette

3 tablespoons red wine vinegar
2 tablespoons Dijon mustard
3/4 teaspoon salt
1/2 teaspoon fresh ground pepper
1/2 cup olive oil
3 medium shallots, minced

Boil potatoes in salted water for 15 to 20 minutes. Drain and cool until slightly warm. Peel and cube potatoes. Toss with white wine and add red pepper.

Whisk together vinegar, mustard, salt, and pepper in a medium-sized bowl until thoroughly blended. Gradually whisk in olive oil to make a thick vinaigrette.

Pour dressing over salad. Add shallots and toss. Chill for 2 to 3 hours to blend flavors.

Bearable Meal Suggestions: Beer and . . . Great with grilled chicken or Pork Steaks (page 92).

DEEP SOUTH POTATO SALAD

PJ explains, "If I'm ever homesick, I make this. If I ever host or attend barbecues, I serve this. A friend of mine once said, 'If all southern food is this good, I'll move there!' I told him, 'It is.'"

8 medium-large potatoes
1 large onion
1/2 green bell pepper
2 to 3 tall celery stalks
8 eggs, hard-boiled
4 tablespoons favorite mustard
1 (16-ounce) jar sweet pickles, diced*
1 (16-ounce) jar mayonnaise
salt and black pepper to taste
2 tablespoons dried basil
2 tablespoons dried parsley
2 tablespoons paprika

Boil potatoes in large stockpot while eggs boil in medium pot. As these boil, dice onion, green pepper, and celery into an extra-large mixing bowl. Soak cooked potatoes and eggs in ice water to cool. Peel and dice eggs and add into mixing bowl with vegetables. Peel and chop potatoes into 3/4-inch cubes and add to mixing bowl. Sprinkle with salt and pepper and begin to mix all ingredients. Add mustard, pickles, and mayonnaise and mix again thoroughly.

Transfer salad into serving bowl and top with basil, parsley, and paprika. Must be refrigerated if not served immediately. Add salt and pepper to taste throughout the mixing of ingredients.

Bearable Meal Suggestions: Beer and . . . Excellent complement to all barbecued meats and Bear Daddy's Baked Beans (page 46). Best served chilled.

---

*Cubed sweet pickles are sold in jars in southern regions of the country—it is not relish. If you cannot find this product in stores in your area, dice sweet gherkins instead.

HOT GERMAN POTATO SALAD

An additional potato salad recipe in a cookbook for Bears seems appropriate. Besides, we knew the name alone would interest you.

3 pounds red potatoes
1 (16-ounce) package polska kielbasa, sliced
6 to 8 slices of bacon
2 to 3 celery stalks, diced
1 large onion, diced

Vinaigrette

1 1/2 tablespoons sugar
1 tablespoon dried mustard
2 teaspoons flour
1/4 cup cider vinegar

Fill a large stockpot with potatoes and water. Bring to a boil over high heat. Cook until tender but slightly resistant when pierced with a fork, 25 to 30 minutes. Drain and let cool slightly, then peel and cut potatoes into 1-inch-thick slices. Place in a large serving bowl.

In a frying pan over medium heat, cook the kielbasa slices through then remove and drain on paper towel. In the same skillet, cook the bacon until crisp. Remove the bacon, crumble, and set aside. Save the drippings in skillet. To the same skillet, add the diced celery and onion, sauté until soft, about 5 minutes. Remove from skillet. Add all sautéed ingredients to bowl with potatoes.

In the same frying pan again, add the sugar, dried mustard, flour, and cider vinegar; cook until the dressing begins to thicken. Pour the dressing over all the ingredients in serving bowl, and mix gently to coat evenly. Serve immediately.

Bearable Meal Suggestions: Beer and . . . Could be considered a side dish but is often served as an entrée.

SWEETY POTATOES ANNA

"Most of my siblings don't like sweet potatoes," Stanley admits, "but they always request my version of this French classic during the holidays."

2 1/2 pounds sweet potatoes, peeled, sliced
1 1/2 cups unsalted butter, melted
freshly ground pepper to taste

Maple Glaze

1/2 cup maple syrup
1/4 cup brown sugar

Preheat oven to 400°F. Butter a 9-inch nonstick cake pan or 10-inch ovenproof frying pan. Starting at center of pan and forming concentric circles, cover bottom with a layer of sweet potatoes, overlapping the slices. Drizzle with some of the melted butter and pepper. Continue layering slices and drizzle remaining butter over top. Butter one side of a piece of aluminum foil large enough to cover the pan, then cover the pan buttered-side down. Place a heavy ovenproof lid (smaller than the pan) on top to weigh down the potato layers. Bake for 40 minutes.

While baking, prepare maple glaze in small saucepan by melting brown sugar with maple syrup over low heat.

Remove lid and foil, and pour maple glaze over baked potatoes. Continue to bake for an additional 30 to 35 minutes, until potatoes are tender and the top is golden.

Remove from oven and cool for 10 minutes. Loosen potatoes from the bottom of pan. Place a flat round platter over the pan and, holding the platter firmly, invert the pan and lift it off. *Note:* excess butter and glaze will flow onto platter. To remove this excess, tilt platter and pour off.

Use Your Tool: A 10-inch ovenproof frying pan is ideal for this recipe.

Bearable Meal Suggestions: Beer and . . . This is a perfect complement to holiday meats, such as turkey or ham.

POTATO AND ONION CASSEROLE

PJ fondly remembers, "This is a favorite dish from my mother's collection. I would always beg her to make this. It's extremely versatile and can work with any kind of meat. From time to time, I crave this enough to make it and enjoy it as its own meal. It's so good!"

6 medium-sized or 4 large potatoes
10 ounces extra-sharp cheddar cheese
1 stick butter
1 large yellow or Vidalia onion
1/2 cup milk
1 cup seasoned bread crumbs

Preheat oven to 375°F. Wash potatoes thoroughly. You may peel or leave skin on, according to preference. Slice potatoes in 1/4-inch rounds (be careful to avoid slicing too thick so they can cook thoroughly). Slice onions and cheese in a similar fashion.

Grease a 2- to 4-quart ovenproof dish or pan and layer bottom with sliced potatoes. Top with a layer of onion, then cheese, and top with several pats of butter. Continue this layering order until you reach the top of pan. Sprinkle with bread crumbs and pour milk evenly in the center and four corners of pan for moistening. Cover and bake for 1 hour. If desired, toast the bread crumb topping until golden brown by removing cover and using the oven broiler for only a few minutes. Watch carefully to prevent burning.

Use Your Tool: This recipe is all about slicing and layering, so use a sharp knife.

Bearable Meal Suggestions: Beer and . . . Perfect with any meat and any vegetable!

PORK STUFFING

"My family waited all year for my mother to make this during the holidays," Stanley recalls. "It was like its own Christmas gift."

1 1/2 pounds bulk pork sausage
1 cup finely chopped celery
1 large onion, chopped
4 Granny Smith apples, peeled, cored, and chopped
2/3 cup walnuts, chopped
2 teaspoons dry sage
1 tablespoon dried parsley
1 teaspoon dried oregano
1 teaspoon dried thyme leaves
1 1/2 teaspoon salt
1/2 teaspoon pepper
2 (12-ounce) packages unseasoned bread cubes
1/4 cup butter, melted
2 cups boiling water

Preheat oven to 375°F. Cook sausage in skillet until no longer pink and drain excess grease.

Combine all ingredients (except for butter and water) in a large mixing bowl. In a small bowl, combine butter and water and pour over ingredients. Toss gently. Spoon mixture into a greased casserole dish and bake for 35 minutes.*

Bearable Meal Suggestions: Beer and . . . This goes perfectly with a grocer's rotisserie turkey or chicken breast for nonholiday meals.

---

*If you choose to stuff a turkey, this recipe will stuff a 15-pound turkey.

CORNMEAL DRESSIN'

This is hands down one of the best examples of hearty Southern cooking. PJ remembers, "I always associate dressing with Thanksgiving and Christmas. It's so easy to make and much better than boxed stuffing."

1 (20-ounce) box of corn bread mix*
1 egg*
1/2 cup milk*
1/2 cup oil*
1 pound bulk sausage, mild or spicy
4 celery stalks
4 green onion stalks
1 large yellow onion
1 large green bell pepper
1 (10-ounce) can soup, cream of mushroom
1 (10-ounce) can soup, cream of chicken
1 (16-ounce) tube sausage, mild or spicy
2 (14-ounce) cans chicken broth

While corn bread is baking in oven, brown the sausage, chop and sauté the vegetables, and add all to large mixing bowl. Add both cream soups to the bowl. When corn bread has finished baking, crumble into same bowl and blend thoroughly. Moisten mixture with 3/4 to 1 can of broth. Add contents of bowl back into cast-iron skillet and bake at 375 degrees for 45 minutes. After 20 minutes, it may be necessary to add an additional 1/2 can of broth to moisten. Use discretion.

Use Your Tool: A 10- to 12-inch cast-iron skillet is ideal for this recipe. If you don't already have one, get one!

Bearable Meal Suggestions: This goes perfectly with a grocer's rotisserie turkey or chicken breast and Sweety Potatoes Anna (page 42). And don't forget the cranberry sauce.

---

*Follow directions on the box of your favorite corn bread mix.

BEAR DADDY'S BAKED BEANS

Another classic side dish that places its emphasis on flavor, not just calories! This is one of those creations perfectly suited for summer barbecues as well as cozy winter suppers.

4 ounces bacon
1 medium-sized onion
1 medium-sized green bell pepper
1 tablespoon oil
3 (28-ounce) cans of baked beans
4 ounces favorite barbecue sauce
1 ounce favorite steak sauce
4 ounces maple syrup

Preheat oven to 300°F. Pan fry or broil bacon until half-cooked, drain and reserve 1 tablespoon of grease.

Chop onion and green pepper and sauté in 1 tablespoon of oil until onion turns translucent. Drain excess liquid from cans of beans and pour into a 10 x 10 x 4-inch baking dish. Add barbecue sauce, steak sauce, syrup, and the tablespoon of reserved bacon grease. Stir all ingredients and add strips of bacon on top. Push bacon down into beans slightly. Bake for 1 hour.

Bearable Meal Suggestions: Beer and . . . Perfect with grilled meats and Deep South Potato Salad (page 40).

No Bear Kitchen
Is Complete Without . . .

VELVEETA

Before there was Cheez Whiz or Kraft Singles or even boxed macaroni and cheese dinners, there was Velveeta. This miraculous cheese food product was introduced to American kitchens in 1928 by Kraft Foods and continues to outsell its competitors.

Although cheese purists scoff at its ingredients—a combination of milk fat, whey, sodium compounds, and food coloring—one can still argue that nothing melts better in the microwave. This cheeselike marvel proves its versatility whether drizzled over a big baked potato and steamed vegetables, blended into your favorite pasta, or used in a dip.

We salute you, Velveeta!

GREEN BEAN CASSEROLE

PJ: "My sister Izzy has mastered this dish. I always hope she will make it for family get-togethers. She is our Green Bean Casserole Queen!"

4 (15-ounce) cans whole green beans
2 (16-ounce) cans meatless chow mein vegetables
2 (10-ounce) cans cream of mushroom or cream of celery soup
1 (7-ounce) can sliced mushrooms
1 pound sharp cheddar, shredded
1 (6-ounce) can french fried onions

Completely drain cans of green beans, chow mein vegetables, and mushrooms. Grease ovenproof baking dish with butter.

Layer the dish with green beans, vegetables, followed by the creamed soup. Next, layer with mushrooms, followed by cheese. Top with the french fried onions. Cover and microwave for 8 to 10 minutes, until cheese looks thoroughly melted. *Note:* If using a very deep casserole dish, halve the amount of each ingredient and layer twice.

Use Your Tool: If you are using a conventional oven, cover with aluminum foil and bake for 20 to 30 minutes at 350 degrees.

Bearable Meal Suggestions: Beer and . . . To turn this recipe into an entrée, add chopped cooked ham or grilled chicken in between the layers.

SESAME GREEN BEANS

If you're looking for something more "gourmet" than traditional green bean casserole, try this delicious recipe. Stanley's friends request it consistently.

1 1/2 teaspoons sesame oil
1 pound fresh green beans
1 1/2 teaspoons soy sauce
1 teaspoon sugar
1 roasted red bell pepper, cut into thin strips
sesame seeds

In a large, nonstick skillet, warm oil over medium heat. Add green beans and stir-fry for 1 to 2 minutes until they begin to soften. Add soy sauce and stir-fry for an additional minute. Add sugar and stir-fry an additional 30 seconds.

Place roasted red bell pepper strips on top of green beans and sprinkle with sesame seeds. Remove from heat, place into a serving dish, and serve.

Use Your Tool: A wok is ideal for this recipe.

Bearable Meal Suggestions: Beer and . . . Serve with Dinner Party Pork Chops (page 94) or Flamin' Flank Steak (page 86).

CORN FRITTERS

Stanley and PJ's dear friend Kathy remembers this dish from her childhood summers in Door County, Wisconsin: "Corn fritters always remind me of wonderfully long summer days, when we would be called for dinner before the sun had the chance to set."

1 can creamed corn
1 egg, beaten
1/4 teaspoon salt
2 to 3 dashes black pepper
1 1/3 cups flour
1 1/2 teaspoons baking powder
4 cups oil

In a bowl, thoroughly mix the creamed corn, egg, salt, pepper, flour, and baking powder. Heat oil in a 3-quart saucepan until hot. Carefully add 1 teaspoon of mixture into the hot oil and fry until golden brown, turning once. Place cooked fritters onto paper towels for drying. Makes approximately 20 fritters.

Use Your Tool: As per the Onion Ring Beer Batter recipe, always be cautious while working with hot oil!

Bearable Meal Suggestions: Beer and . . . A wonderful side dish to accompany Pork Steaks (page 92), Slow-Simmered Country Ribs (page 93), or Sweet Hot Chili (page 72).

No Bear Kitchen Is Complete Without . . .

CORNFLAKES

Remember the first time you poured your cornflakes into a mixing bowl instead of a cereal bowl for breakfast? For decades, Americans graced these golden flakes with a variety of favorite toppings until their creativity reached its apex. Cornflakes leaped out of the cereal bowl and onto the dinner table the first time it was crumbled on top of a baked casserole—and there was no turning back!

This versatile cereal has come a long way from its original invention in 1894 by Dr. John Harvey Kellogg and his brother Will Keith Kellogg in Battle Creek, Michigan. Today, Kellogg's Corn Flakes cereal can be used in everything from cookies and pies to meatballs and meat loaves. If you're tempted to experiment, visit the Kellogg's Web site at <www.kelloggs.com> for more great ideas!

EASY CHEESY POTATO BAKE

This is a signature dish of Stanley's sister, Sheila, and a classic side for any occasion. What makes it a classic? Notice a stick of butter and the can of soup—true characteristics of "comfort food."

1 pound frozen hash browns
8 ounces sour cream
1 (10-ounce) can cream of mushroom soup
1 1/2 sticks butter, melted
8 to 12 ounces cheddar cheese, shredded
2 cups cornflakes, crushed

Preheat oven to 350°F. In a bowl, mix frozen hash browns, sour cream, and cream of mushroom soup. Pour mixture into a large oven-proof baking dish. Pour half of the melted butter over mixture. Add cheese evenly over top, followed by the cornflakes. Pour remaining butter over top. Bake for 30 minutes.

Use Your Tool: Use a large oval or rectangular casserole dish.

Bearable Meal Suggestions: Beer and . . . This is perfect with any meat and/or vegetable entrée.

CABIN FEVER SOUP

Is cold, miserable weather keeping you inside? Then it's time for soup! Besides, what could be better during hibernation?

12 1/2 cups (or more) canned chicken broth
1 1/4 cups wild rice (approximately 7 1/2 ounces)
6 cups frozen corn kernels, thawed
2 tablespoons vegetable oil
10 ounces fully cooked smoked sausage, cut into half cubes
3 carrots, peeled and diced
2 medium onions, chopped
1 1/2 cups half-and-half
Fresh chives or parsley, chopped

Bring 5 cups broth to simmer in medium saucepan over medium heat. Add wild rice and simmer until all liquid evaporates and rice is almost tender, stirring occasionally, about 40 minutes.

In the meantime, puree 4 cups corn and 1 1/2 cups chicken broth in processor or blender until thick and almost smooth. Heat vegetable oil in large stockpot over medium-high heat. Add sausage and sauté until beginning to brown, about 5 minutes. Add carrots and onions and stir 3 minutes. Add remaining 6 cups chicken broth and bring soup to simmer. Reduce heat to low and simmer soup 15 minutes.

Add cooked wild rice, corn puree, and remaining 2 cups corn kernels to soup. Cook until wild rice is very tender and flavors blend, about 15 minutes longer. Mix in half-and-half. Thin soup with more chicken broth if desired. Season soup with salt and pepper. Ladle soup into bowls and decorate with chives or parsley.

Use Your Tool: Use a food processor or blender for best results in making the corn and broth base.

Bearable Meal Suggestions: Beer and . . . Serve with Corn Fritters (page 51) or Scratch Biscuits (page 25).

WHAT'S IT ALL ABOUT ... ALFREDO

"This is one of the easiest and most delicious pasta recipes I know," Stanley admits. "It's a perfect meal for entertaining because it's so convenient and impressive."

4 tablespoons butter
8 ounces heavy cream
2 1/2 cups parmesan cheese, freshly grated
1 pound rigatoni pasta
black pepper, freshly ground

Melt the butter in a saucepan; add the cream and half the cheese. Keep warm.

Cook the pasta in a large stockpot, following package directions carefully to avoid overcooking. Drain the pasta and return to stockpot. Stir remaining cheese into pasta and blend thoroughly. When every piece is coated, stir in the cream sauce. Add freshly ground black pepper to taste and serve at once.

Bearable Meal Suggestions: Beer and . . . Serve with grilled Italian sausage and garlic bread.

POTATOES CHANTAL

"My French mother wasn't the type to constantly cook French foods, but when she did, they were extraordinary," PJ recalls. "This is so easy—it will change your mind about ordinary mashed potatoes!"

5 pounds Yukon Gold or baking potatoes
1 bunch fresh parsley, finely chopped
1 pint half-and-half
1/2 cup butter
salt and pepper

Peel and boil potatoes in an 8-quart boiler. While potatoes are boiling, pull parsley from stems and chop very fine.

Begin mashing potatoes with one cup of half-and-half, 1/4 cup of butter (half a stick), and a heavy dash of salt and pepper. Then add a handful of parsley and continue to mash and blend.

Repeat this procedure with the remaining half-and-half and butter. The rest is left to your preference. Begin to taste and add additional parsley, salt, and pepper, if desired. Continue to mash to desired consistency.

Use Your Tool: Here's your chance to show off your Bear strength and finally use that potato masher sitting in your kitchen drawer.

Bearable Meal Suggestions: Beer and . . . Terrific with barbecued meats or hamburgers!

MANLY, YES—MACARONI SALAD

Tired of eating that lousy premade macaroni salad from the supermarket deli? Instead, make a fresh, easy, affordable, Bear-size portion yourself. Once you've mastered this easy recipe you'll be sure to
experiment—get creative and it will never be boring.

20 ounces macaroni
1 small onion, chopped
1/4 cup green pepper, chopped
1 cup celery, chopped
5 carrots, shredded
1 pint mayonnaise
1 can sweetened condensed milk
3/4 cup vinegar
1 1/2 cup sugar

Cook macaroni in medium-large stockpot, stirring occasionally.
As macaroni boils, chop onion, green pepper, and celery, and add to a
large mixing bowl. Shred or chop carrots and add to bowl.

When macaroni reaches desired tenderness, drain and soak in cold
water until chilled. Drain again thoroughly to remove as much water
as possible. Pour into mixing bowl with the chopped vegetables. Add
mayonnaise, sweetened condensed milk, vinegar, and sugar. Blend
thoroughly and serve or chill and allow flavors to blend.

Use Your Tool: A food processor will make chopping much faster and
easier.

Bearable Meal Suggestions: Beer and . . . Another terrific side dish for
summer meats such as Husbear Burgers (page 83), Grandma's Barbecue Beef (page 84), or Slow-Simmered Country Ribs (page 93).

SECTION IV:
COME-AND-GET-IT ENTRÉES

CHEESY CHICKEN CASSEROLE

This recipe epitomizes the Bear comfort food—easy to make and completely satisfying, especially with hot baked corn bread. Look for our secret to better-tasting corn bread below!

8 boneless chicken breasts
1 (16-ounce) package Velveeta, sliced
1 cup cream of chicken soup
1/4 cup white wine (optional)
1 cup herb stuffing mix, crushed
1/4 cup butter or margarine, melted

Preheat oven to 350°F. In a 9 x 13-inch lightly greased pan, place chicken on bottom and top with sliced cheese. Combine soup and wine and spoon evenly over chicken and cheese. Top with crushed stuffing mix, then drizzle melted butter or margarine over stuffing crumbs. Bake for 1 hour.

Use Your Tool: When using a packaged corn bread mix, substitute creamed corn in place of milk—it guarantees a moist corn bread!

Bearable Meal Suggestions: Beer and corn bread.

JOHNNY BEAR-ZETTI

This is a play on a hearty Midwestern favorite. Don't just boil your pasta—bake it, too!

2 bacon slices, chopped
1 pound ground beef
1 (4-ounce) can sliced mushrooms
1 (8-ounce) can tomato sauce
1 (12-ounce) can tomato paste
1/2 cup celery, diced
1 garlic clove, chopped
1 onion, finely chopped
1 green pepper, finely chopped
1/2 box thin spaghetti, cooked
1/4 pound cheddar cheese, sliced

Preheat oven to 350°F. In a large skillet, fry bacon and ground beef until cooked, then drain. Add all other ingredients to skillet except pasta and cheese; mix together to consistent texture. Boil and drain pasta thoroughly. In a large casserole dish, layer from the bottom: pasta, meat sauce mixture, and sliced cheese. Repeat layering until all amounts are used. Bake for 1 hour.

Bearable Meal Suggestions: Beer and corn bread.

SPAGHETTI CARBONARA

"Usually, the traditional carbonara recipe is more complicated than this," Stanley admits. "I love making this version—it's simpler without sacrificing flavor."

10 slices bacon, cut into half-inch wide pieces
1 pound thin spaghetti
1 box frozen peas
4 egg yolks
1 cup whipping cream
5 tablespoons parmesan cheese, grated
salt and pepper to season

Bring large pot of water to boil. In the meantime, cook bacon in a large skillet until crisp. Remove bacon to dry and drain skillet of excess fat, leaving a thin coat in skillet. Cook pasta and peas in boiling water until pasta is done, being careful not to overcook the pasta. Whisk together egg yolks, cream, and cheese.

Drain pasta and add it to the bacon pan. Add bacon and egg mixture and place over medium heat. Toss ingredients with tongs to coat and distribute ingredients evenly. Add salt and pepper to taste, then serve.

Use Your Tool: Set aside a cup of the pasta water before draining, in case your cream sauce is too thick.

Bearable Meal Suggestions: Beer and a nice, hearty Italian bread.

(SQUEAL LIKE A) PIGGY MAC

Here's an updated version of a childhood classic—not that we don't still enjoy the "blue box and powder."

1 pound elbow macaroni
4 tablespoons butter
8 ounces heavy cream
2 1/2 cups grated parmesan cheese
1 cup cooked ham, diced
black pepper to taste

In large pot, bring water to boil for pasta. In the meantime, melt butter in a pan and add the cream and half the cheese. Stir until blended and add ham. Stir and keep warm. Cook the pasta without overcooking, drain thoroughly, then stir in remaining cheese. Add ham sauce until pasta is thoroughly coated. Add black pepper to taste and serve.

Use Your Tool: Freshly grated parmesan cheese is ideal.

Bearable Meal Suggestions: Beer.

CREOLE BEANS AND SAUSAGE

Stanley notes, "This was always requested by my friends when we celebrated Mardi Gras in the Soulard area of St. Louis. This gave us the energy to throw a lot of beads off my rooftop."

1/4 cup olive oil
1 cup onion, finely chopped
1 cup green bell pepper, finely chopped
1 cup red bell pepper, finely chopped
1 teaspoon fresh garlic, minced
1/2 teaspoon dried oregano
2 cups cooked country sausage, diced
1 cup beef stock
3 cups tomato sauce
1/2 cup sherry
1/4 teaspoon black pepper
1/4 teaspoon cayenne pepper
4 cups cooked red beans
Tabasco to taste
Cooked rice

Heat oil in large skillet. Add onion, bell peppers, garlic, oregano, and sausage. Cook until vegetables are tender. Add remaining ingredients except beans and rice and bring to a boil. Reduce heat and simmer for 10 minutes. Add beans and bring to a boil. Remove from heat. Season with Tabasco to taste and serve over rice.

Bearable Meal Suggestions: Beer and King Cake (Ask any Mardi Gras fanatic—who's got the baby?)

BEEF STROGANOFF

Beef, cream, butter, beer . . . what more could a Bear want from an entrée?

12 ounces wide egg noodles
6 tablespoons butter
3 pounds beef tenderloin or cubed steak, cut into bite-sized pieces
1 cup beer
1/4 cup shallots, chopped
1 pound small button mushrooms, thickly sliced
1 cup canned beef broth
3/4 cup heavy whipping cream
1 tablespoon Dijon mustard
1 tablespoon fresh dill, chopped
1 tablespoon paprika
Salt and pepper to taste

Prepare noodles according to package directions and drain. Transfer to bowl and add 4 tablespoons butter and toss to coat. Season with salt and pepper.

Sprinkle meat with salt and pepper. In a large skillet, add beer and meat and simmer over high heat until meat is tender. Remove meat and juices from pan when browned. Set aside.

Melt 2 tablespoons of butter in same skillet over medium-high heat. Add shallots and cook until tender, about 2 minutes. Add mushrooms and sprinkle with pepper; sauté about 10 minutes. Add beef broth and simmer until liquid thickens and coats back of spoon, about 14 minutes. Stir in heavy cream and mustard. Add meat and its juices to pan. Simmer over medium-low heat until meat is heated through, about 2 minutes. Stir in fresh dill. Season to taste with salt and pepper. Divide noodles onto serving plates. Ladle beef sauce over noodles, generously sprinkle with paprika, and serve.

Bearable Meal Suggestions: Beer or a nice red wine.

GARLIC CHICKEN STROGANOFF

One Stroganoff recipe isn't enough for this book. This one's for garlic lovers!

1 teaspoon olive oil
1 large onion, chopped
8 ounces fresh mushrooms, sliced
1 teaspoon minced garlic
4 boneless/skinless chicken breast halves, bite-sized
1 (12-ounce) box fettuccine noodles
16 ounces frozen broccoli florets
2 tablespoons dry sherry
1 (10-ounce) can cream of mushroom soup
1 cup sour cream
1 teaspoon Worcestershire sauce
1 tablespoon paprika
black pepper to taste

Begin by setting a large pot of water to boil for the pasta.

Heat oil over medium heat in a large (12-inch) skillet. Add onion, mushrooms, and garlic; stir occasionally. Add chicken to skillet and raise the heat. Cook until chicken is no longer pink in the center, stirring occasionally.

Add fettuccine to boiling water and cook 5 to 10 minutes. Add broccoli to the pot and cook several more minutes until pasta is tender.

When chicken is fully cooked, add sherry and soup. Reduce heat and stir well. Add sour cream and Worcestershire sauce and stir.

Drain pasta and broccoli thoroughly and place on individual plates. Top plates with chicken sauce and sprinkle generously with paprika and black pepper. Serve immediately.

FIERY CHICKEN ENCHILADAS

One bite of these bad boys will make you think you've landed south of the border! Can you take the heat?

4 ounces cream cheese, softened
1/4 cup sour cream
2 cups favorite brand/flavor salsa
2 cups cheddar or Jack cheese, shredded
2 cups chicken, cooked and shredded
1 cup corn, thawed if frozen
1/2 teaspoon cumin
1/4 teaspoon cayenne
8 large, fresh jalapeños, diced
salt and pepper
12 soft flour or corn tortillas (6- to 8-inch size)

Preheat oven to 325°F. In a large bowl, blend cream cheese and sour cream. Stir in 1/2 cup of salsa and 1 cup of grated cheese. In a different bowl, mix the chicken, corn, cumin, cayenne, jalapeño, salt, and pepper. Add chicken mixture to the cheese mixture and stir.

In a baking dish, spread 1/2 cup of salsa over the bottom. Place approximately 1/3 cup of filling on a tortilla, roll, and place in dish with the seam side down. Repeat process with the remaining tortillas. Pour the rest of the salsa over top, followed by the remaining shredded cheese. Bake for 25 minutes.

Use Your Tool: Regulate the degree of heat by adjusting the type of salsa and the amounts of cayenne and jalapeño.

Bearable Meal Suggestions: Beer. Ice-cold beer.

No Bear Kitchen Is Complete Without . . .

CREAM OF MUSHROOM SOUP

We believe this to be without a doubt the most incredible food invention ever created. The Campbell Soup Company blessed the world with their Cream of Mushroom Soup in 1934—the same year they introduced Chicken with Noodles (later Chicken Noodle) Soup. As a testimony to its versatility, you'll find many of our recipes include it as an important base ingredient.

In fact, according to the folks at <www.campbellsoup.com>, "Cooking with soup remains so popular that Americans use more than 440 million cans each year in a variety of easy-to-prepare recipes. Campbell's Soup ranks behind only meat/poultry, pasta, and seasonings/spices as the ingredient most often used to prepare dinner each evening."

This must be stocked in your Bear pantry at all times. You'll be sure to use it!

TUNA RICE SKILLET

This is a terrific spin on a classic tuna casserole idea. "I like it for its simplicity . . . this allows for a great deal of experimentation if you're interested," PJ says.

1 cup white rice, cooked
1 can cream of mushroom soup
1 (12-ounce) can tuna, drained
1 (15-ounce) can peas, drained
black pepper to taste

In a medium saucepan, cook rice as directed. Once cooked, add soup, tuna, and peas to saucepan and stir. Remove from heat and cover for 5 minutes. Add pepper and stir. Serve at once.

Use Your Tool: Try substituting chicken for tuna.

Bearable Meal Suggestions: Beer. Also serve with hot baked bread or dinner rolls.

SWEET HOT CHILI

"This recipe has been in my family for years," Stanley recalls. "It's a unique recipe in that it tastes sweet when you begin eating it, and then you feel the fire as it goes down."

1 (16-ounce) box rigatoni pasta
2 tablespoons olive oil
1 yellow onion, diced
1 red pepper, diced
2 pounds ground beef
1 pound bulk pork sausage
1 (40-ounce) can Chili Hot Beans
1 (14-ounce) can diced tomatoes, drained
1 (1-ounce) package chili seasoning
1 teaspoon cayenne pepper
2 tablespoons ground cumin
1 (14-ounce) can tomato sauce
1 cup brown sugar, firmly packed

Prepare pasta per box directions, drain, and set aside. In a large sauté pan, add olive oil, onion, red peppers, and sauté 5 to 7 minutes. Then, in same pan, add ground beef and sausage and brown thoroughly. To meat mixture, add beans, diced tomatoes, chili seasoning, cayenne pepper, cumin, tomato sauce, and brown sugar. Mix thoroughly and simmer for 30 minutes. Pour meat mixture over cooked pasta and mix completely.

Use Your Tool: Adjust heat of chili by using more or less cayenne pepper.

Bearable Meal Suggestions: Beer and corn bread.

POLAR BEAR CHILI

4 whole boneless, skinless chicken breasts
4 1/2 cups water
2 tablespoons olive oil
2 cups onions, finely chopped
4 garlic cloves, minced
6 jalapeño chilies, cored, seeded, and minced
3 teaspoons ground cumin
1 1/2 teaspoons dried oregano
1/2 teaspoon cayenne pepper
2 (14-ounce) cans Great Northern (white) beans
6 cups chicken stock
2 cups Monterey Jack cheese, grated

In a large skillet, place chicken breasts in the water and cover. Simmer on low heat for 30 minutes or until chicken is opaque throughout. Remove chicken and reserve the cooking liquid. Once chicken has cooled enough, shred into bite-sized pieces.

In a large stockpot, heat oil over medium heat. Add the onions and cook about 10 minutes. Add garlic, chilies, cumin, oregano, and cayenne pepper, and cook a few minutes longer. Add the beans, chicken stock, and reserved cooking liquid, and bring to a boil. Cover, reduce heat, and simmer for 2 hours, stirring occasionally. Add salt to taste. Before serving, add shredded chicken and grated cheese.

Bearable Meal Suggestions: Beer and hot Corn Fritters (page 51).

CHINESE CHICKEN SALAD

This is one of our "lighter" recipes, which means you can eat more of it!

1 (8-ounce) package wonton skins
3 cups vegetable oil
3 chicken breasts
1/4 cup soy sauce
1/4 cup sugar
1 head iceberg lettuce, chopped
2 (8-ounce) cans water chestnuts, drained and sliced
1 (6-ounce) can black olives, drained and chopped
1 bunch green onions, chopped

Dressing:

1/2 cup sugar
1/2 cup rice wine vinegar
1/2 cup olive oil

To prepare wontons: In large, deep skillet (or deep fryer set at 360°F), heat vegetable oil. Gently place wonton skins in hot oil. Be careful not to add too many at a time. Fry until deep golden and crisp. Remove immediately and lay out to dry on paper towels. Repeat procedure until all skins are cooked.

To poach chicken: In a large sauté pan, cover chicken breasts with water. Add soy sauce and sugar and bring to a boil. Reduce to simmer and cook approximately 30 minutes or until chicken is no longer pink in center. Remove from pan and cool. Shred chicken into bite-sized pieces.

To prepare salad: In large bowl, combine lettuce, water chestnuts, black olives, green onions, and chicken. Toss ingredients thoroughly.

To prepare dressing: Combine dressing ingredients and whisk until sugar is dissolved. Pour dressing over salad mixture and crumble fried wontons into salad. Toss and serve.

Use Your Tool: This recipe will definitely test your prep skills. It's worth the effort!

CURRY CHICKEN SALAD

3 chicken breasts
2 cups of water
1 cup apple juice
1/2-inch piece of fresh ginger
1/4 cup honey-roasted peanuts
2 Granny Smith apples, cored and diced
1 cup seedless grapes, cut in half
mixed greens

Dressing

1/4 cup rice wine vinegar
1 tablespoon fresh ginger, grated
2 cloves garlic, minced
2 shallots, minced
1 tablespoon curry powder
1 tablespoon sugar
2/3 cup mayonnaise
soy sauce to taste

Place chicken breasts in a sauté pan, add water, apple juice, and piece of ginger. Poach chicken until cooked all the way through. Remove, let cool, and shred chicken.

Make dressing by combining all ingredients in a blender or food processor. In a large bowl, toss chicken, nuts, apples, and grapes with half the dressing.

Toss greens in another bowl with the remaining dressing. Arrange the chicken mixture on the greens and serve.

CUB SALAD

This is a great side dish recipe for summer buffet tables—especially barbecues and potluck events. It also makes a delicious entrée by adding grilled chicken or pork!

2 packages ramen noodles, chicken flavored
1/2 cup sliced almonds
1 (16-ounce) bag coleslaw mix
1/2 cup scallions
1/2 cup sunflower seeds (kernels without shells)
3/4 cup oil
1/2 cup white or rice wine vinegar
2 packets ramen noodle chicken flavor seasoning
1/2 cup sugar
Seedless red or white grapes (optional)

Preheat oven to 350°F. Break apart ramen noodles and boil for 3 minutes in medium saucepan. Spread sliced almonds on a cookie sheet and toast in the oven for 3 to 5 minutes. Drain and cool noodles, and add to large mixing bowl. Add coleslaw mix, toasted almonds, scallions, grapes, and sunflower seeds; then blend.

In a separate sealed container, mix oil, vinegar, seasoning mix, and sugar. Pour over dry ingredients and blend thoroughly. Chill before serving.

Bearable Meal Suggestions: Beer. As a side dish, serve with Husbear Burgers (page 83) or Slow-Simmered Country Ribs (page 93).

SWEET PEPPER SALAD

Like our other salads, this stands on its own as an impressive side dish. It could also be tossed with grilled chicken for a satisfying entrée.

1 pound rigatoni pasta
1 red bell pepper, cut into julienne strips
1 yellow bell pepper, cut into julienne strips
1 (10-ounce) package shredded (matchstick) carrots
8 ounces favorite brand Italian dressing
3 to 4 tablespoons sugar
Salt and pepper to taste

Boil pasta per instructions on box and drain thoroughly. In a large mixing bowl, combine peppers, carrots, and pasta. In a sealed container, combine dressing and sugar, and shake until sugar dissolves. Pour over pasta mixture and blend thoroughly. Chill for at least 2 hours and serve.

Bearable Meal Suggestions: Beer.

WHAT-A-CROCK-POT STEW

Oh, the mighty beef stew. Bears know it and love it. Although a Crock-Pot is ideal for a recipe like this, we offer a convenient, classic stove top alternative—created entirely in one pot. Enjoy!

6 slices bacon
2 pounds beef round, cubed
1/2 cup cooking sherry
2 garlic cloves, chopped
1 teaspoon dried rosemary
1 bay leaf
1/2 cup water
6 carrots, peeled and cut chunky style
2 onions, peeled and cut chunky style
1 (10-ounce) box peas, frozen
salt and pepper to taste

Using a large pot, fry bacon and remove. Brown beef in bacon fat and remove. Drain pot of excess fat, leaving a portion to coat the bottom. Add sherry to same pot over a medium heat. Return beef back to the pot, along with garlic, seasonings, and water. Cover and bring to a boil; then reduce to low heat and simmer for 1 hour, stirring occasionally. Add bacon, carrots, onions, and peas, and bring to a boil again; then reduce heat to low and simmer for 45 minutes. Remove bay leaf and serve.

Bearable Meal Suggestions: Beer and hot buttered bread.

BRAT BAKE

It is no surprise that Bears are attracted to bratwurst . . . some reasons are more obvious than others.

1 cup celery, chopped
1 cup onion, chopped
4 (12-ounce) bratwurst, cut into 1-inch pieces
4 medium potatoes, peeled and sliced
1 (16-ounce) can green beans, drained
1 (10-ounce) can cream of garlic chicken soup
1/2 cup milk

Preheat oven at 375°F. In a frying pan, sauté celery and onion until partially cooked, then place into mixing bowl. In same pan, cook brat pieces thoroughly and drain excess fat.

In a well-buttered casserole dish, place thinly sliced potatoes and top with cooked brat. Top with green beans, celery, and onion. Blend soup and milk well, and pour over all ingredients. Bake for 90 minutes.

Bearable Meal Suggestions: Beer and a side order of Corn Fritters (page 51).

SECTION V:
BEAR MEAT

HUSBEAR BURGERS

"I'm so grateful to have parents who love food and who taught me to appreciate food flavor. They always knew how to take ordinary food and make it more interesting," PJ recalls. "This burger recipe is an excellent example. It never fails to impress at a cookout."

4 pounds ground sirloin
1/2 medium-sized onion, finely chopped
1/2 medium-sized bell pepper, finely chopped
1/2 cup Worcestershire sauce
1/2 cup red wine
1 cup seasoned bread crumbs
1 tablespoon salt
1 tablespoon black pepper
1 egg

In a large mixing bowl, combine all ingredients. Pull apart a palm-sized section and begin patting and forming beef mixture into a patty shape, approximately 1/2-inch thick and 4 inches in diameter. If mixture seems too moist, you can add additional bread crumbs. If too dry, moisten with additional wine.

Place formed patties on cookie sheet, separating layers of patties with waxed paper sheets. Refrigerate until ready to grill or skillet fry. Makes approximately 10 to 12 burgers.

Use Your Tool: Your best tool for this recipe? Your own two clean Bear paws—dig in and have fun!

Bearable Meal Suggestions: Beer. Ideally served with Deep South Potato Salad (page 40) and Bear Daddy's Baked Beans (page 46).

GRANDMA'S BARBECUE BEEF

"Every time I visited my grandmother, I couldn't wait for her to serve this dish," Stanley reminisces.

2 tablespoons olive oil
1 large onion, chopped
2 (12-ounce) cans corned beef
3 pounds ground beef
1 small bottle chili sauce
4 tablespoons brown sugar
2 tablespoons vinegar
1 tablespoon chili powder
1 (8-count) package hamburger buns

In stockpot, heat olive oil and sauté onions until translucent, approximately 7 minutes. Add corned beef and ground beef; brown thoroughly. Add chili sauce, brown sugar, vinegar, and chili powder. Combine well and let simmer for 30 to 45 minutes on low heat, stirring occasionally. Serve open faced on hamburger buns.

Bearable Meal Suggestions: Beer and Deep South Potato Salad (page 40).

FUR-OCIOUS POT ROAST

WOOF! This comfort food classic is so easy and guaranteed to keep your Crock-Pot in use year-round.

1 (2-to-3 pound) boneless beef chuck pot roast
2 tablespoons cooking oil
10 to 12 ounces medium potatoes, peeled and quartered
6 large carrots, coarsely chopped
2 small onions, quartered
3 celery stalks, cut into 1-inch pieces
3/4 cup red wine
1 tablespoon Worcestershire sauce
1 teaspoon instant beef bouillon, crushed
1 teaspoon basil, dried and crushed

Trim fat from roast. In a 4- to 6-quart pot, brown roast on all sides in hot oil. Drain off fat. Place chopped vegetables in a 4-quart Crock-Pot. Place roast on top of vegetables. Combine wine, Worcestershire sauce, bouillon, and basil, and pour over meat. Cover and cook on low heat for 10 to 12 hours.

Use Your Tool: Make sure you have a Crock-Pot large enough to handle your roast. If not, cut your roast to fit.

Bearable Meal Suggestions: Beer.

FLAMIN' FLANK STEAK

Flank steak is the best cut of beef for a marinade. It allows the flavor to penetrate completely. However, other cuts of beef—such as T-bone and rib eye—can also be used.

2 tablespoons fresh lime juice
grated zest of 1 lime
2 cloves garlic, minced
3/4 teaspoon hot chili oil
1/4 cup vegetable oil
1 teaspoon red pepper flakes
1/4 teaspoon cayenne pepper
1/2 cup red wine
1 tablespoon sugar
2 tablespoons soy sauce
1 to 2 pounds flank steak

Combine all ingredients, except flank steak, in a small bowl. Place meat in a shallow sealable container. Pour mixture over meat and cover. Refrigerate for at least 2 hours, but all day is better. Turn meat occasionally and baste with the marinade.

Remove meat from marinade (reserve the marinade) and place on hot grill. Cook for 10 to 12 minutes, turning once and brushing several times with reserved marinade. This dish is best served rare.

Bearable Meal Suggestions: Beer and Yankee Potato Salad (page 39).

UNCLE BEAU'S STANDING RIB (BIG MEAT)

Our dear friend Beau was kind enough to share the secret to his Big
Meat. Thank you, sir.

1 standing rib roast (3 ribs minimum)
4 cloves fresh garlic, peeled and sliced
fresh thyme, several sprigs
1/4 cup whole black peppercorns
4 tablespoons (1/2 stick) unsalted butter, softened
3 medium onions, quartered
4 shallots
kosher salt to taste

Preheat oven to 350°F. Rinse your meat well under cold running
water and pat dry with paper towels. Cut several small 1-inch deep
slits into the top of the roast with a small sharp knife. Insert a slice of
garlic and a small sprig of thyme into each slit. Liberally season the
entire roast with the kosher salt. In a spice grinder or a food processor
(or use the back of a heavy pan if you're feeling butch) pulse or crush
the peppercorns into very coarse pieces. Press the peppercorns into
all surfaces of the roast to form a crust. (This is called "au poivre," for
those of you who want to wow your guests with your culinary acu-
men.) Finally, rub the entire roast with the softened butter.

Place the roast on a rack in a roasting pan and arrange the onions,
shallots, and remaining thyme in the space under the ribs and on the
sides of your roast. These aromatics will perfume your beef and are
delicious served alongside the finished product.

Roast your meat for 20 to 25 minutes per pound at 350°F or until
the internal temperature reads 125°F for medium rare. Make sure you
let the roast rest for at least 20 minutes before carving to prevent the
juices from gushing out early. Nobody likes that. (wink)

BEEF OR CHICKEN FAJITAS

Feel like a gourmet without the work. This marinade is guaranteed to impress any dinner guest.

Marinade

1/4 cup fresh lime juice
1 jalapeño chili, seeded and diced
1 tablespoon cumin
2 garlic cloves, minced
2 tablespoons vegetable oil
1/2 cup beer
1/4 tablespoon cayenne pepper

Fajitas

1 flank steak (approximately 2 pounds) or 6 boneless, skinless
    chicken breast halves
12 flour tortillas
salt and pepper to taste
2 tablespoons vegetable oil
1 red bell pepper, cored, seeded, and sliced julienne style
1 green bell pepper, cored, seeded, and sliced julienne style
1 cup red onion, thinly sliced

Mix all marinade ingredients in a bowl and set aside. In a shallow nonaluminum dish, pour marinade over steak or chicken. Marinate at room temperature for 2 hours or cover and refrigerate overnight.

Preheat oven to 350°F, then light charcoal or gas grill. Wrap stack of tortillas tightly in aluminum foil and place in oven for 15 to 20 minutes or until warm. Remove meat from marinade and season with salt and pepper. Grill steak for 10 to 15 minutes per side, or grill chicken for approximately 5 minutes per side. Remove all meat from heat and slice diagonally across the grain into thin slices. Keep warm.

In a skillet over high heat, add oil, pepper strips, and onions; sauté until vegetables are tender and slightly caramelized, approximately 5 minutes. Add meat to skillet and combine until heated thoroughly.

Serve with warm tortillas, guacamole, salsa, diced tomatoes, grated Jack cheese, and refried beans (pinto or black).

MOM'S MEAT LOAF

"What can I say about my mother's meat loaf?" PJ asks. "It is my favorite ground beef recipe. She always bakes and wraps a hot one for me to take home after a visit. Believe me, an airplane flight can seem eternal when you pack a hot meat loaf in your carry-on bag."

3 pounds lean ground chuck
1/2 green bell pepper, chopped
1 medium onion, chopped
2 cloves garlic, minced
2 eggs
2 slices bread
1 cup red wine
1 cup milk
1/2 teaspoon dried oregano
1/2 teaspoon dried thyme
1/2 teaspoon parsley flakes
1 teaspoon salt
1 teaspoon black pepper

Preheat oven to 325°F. In a large bowl, mix meat, green pepper, onion, and garlic. Add eggs and blend. Soak bread in wine, crumble, and add to mixture. Add spices, salt, black pepper, and milk; mix well. Mold mixture into loaf shape and place in large covered baking pan. Bake for 75 minutes, or until liquid runs clear from loaf.

Use Your Tool: Like the Husbear Burgers (page 83) recipe, use your own two clean Bear paws—dig in and have fun!

Bearable Meal Suggestions: Beer. If served hot, enjoy with Potatoes Chantal (page 57) or Easy Cheesy Potato Bake (page 53). If served cold, slice loaf on hearty white or wheat bread and top with plenty of mayonnaise and mustard.

No Bear Kitchen
Is Complete Without . . .

GROUND BEEF

Let's see. You can find it on tacos, or piled onto a pizza. You can find it in a bun, layered in a casserole, or stuffed in a pie crust. You can mold it into patties or into a loaf.

You can season it, mold it, brown it, mix it, smother it, bake it, fry it, grill it, smoke it, sauce it, nuke it, or crumble it . . . and that's just the beginning.

We salute ground beef—because Bears wouldn't be Bears without it!

PORK STEAKS

3 to 4 pound pork shoulder or pork butt, cut in 1-inch-thick steaks
1 cup butter, melted

Sauce

1 cup favorite barbecue sauce
2/3 cup honey
2 tablespoons Worcestershire sauce
2 teaspoons garlic salt
1 teaspoon prepared mustard

In a small bowl, combine all the sauce ingredients and mix well.

Place steaks on a grill about 4 inches above the coals or on a medium-low gas heat. Cook the steaks about 8 minutes per side—brushing them with butter with every turn on the grill. After cooking, brush with sauce and continue cooking an additional 5 minutes, turning and brushing with sauce.

SLOW-SIMMERED COUNTRY RIBS

Here's some animal trivia for you: Did you know that a pig's rib is bigger and meatier than a cow's rib? Some Bears may already know this, of course.

6 pounds country pork ribs
2 (16-ounce) bottles of beer
4 cups favorite barbecue sauce

In a large stockpot, boil ribs in beer about 10 minutes. In a large (preferably 13 x 9 x 3-inch) all-purpose disposable aluminum pan, pour 2 cups of barbecue sauce into the bottom. Place ribs into pan and pour remaining sauce over them. Cover with foil and place on center of grill. *Note:* For gas grill, cook on low heat for 35 to 40 minutes. For charcoal grill, use indirect heat for 20 to 25 minutes.

Use Your Tool: We recommend the previously mentioned disposable pan for easy cleanup!

Bearable Meal Suggestions: Beer and Easy Cheesy Potato Bake (page 53).

DINNER PARTY PORK CHOPS

Show your friends that you can do more in the kitchen than microwave your meals. Even a novice cook can handle this impressive recipe.

2 teaspoons vegetable oil
4 (1-inch) boneless, center-cut pork chops, trimmed
salt and pepper
3 tablespoons cider vinegar
2 tablespoons sugar
2/3 cup white wine
2/3 cup chicken stock
3 firm, ripe pears, peeled, cored, and cut lengthwise into eighths
1 piece fresh ginger (2 inches long), peeled and cut into julienne
   strips
2 teaspoons cornstarch

In a large skillet, heat oil over medium-high heat. Add pork chops and cook for 3 to 5 minutes per side or until just browned; season lightly with salt and pepper. Remove from pan and keep warm.

In same pan, add vinegar and sugar, stirring to dissolve the sugar. Cook over heat approximately 1 minute or until syrup turns a dark amber color. Pour in wine and chicken stock; cook, stirring for about 30 seconds. Add pears and ginger, and cook uncovered for about 5 minutes or until pears are tender.

Dissolve cornstarch into teaspoons of water and whisk into pear sauce (sauce will thicken almost immediately). Reduce heat to low and return pork to skillet. Simmer gently for about 2 minutes.

Use Your Tool: We recommend a large (6-quart) sauté pan for this recipe.

Bearable Meal Suggestions: Beer, Potato and Onion Casserole (page 43), and Sesame Green Beans (page 50).

RUSSIAN RIVER OVEN-BAKED FISH

Inspired by a trip to Lazy Bear Weekend in California, this yummy meal is ideal for sharing on warm, leisurely summer evenings—preferably near an open fire with someone special . . . followed by breath mints.

1 pound fresh or frozen skinless cod, orange roughy, or catfish
    fillets (1/2-inch thick)
1/4 cup buttermilk
1/4 cup all-purpose flour
1/3 cup fine Italian-seasoned bread crumbs
1/4 cup parmesan cheese, grated
1/2 teaspoon dried dill
2 tablespoons butter, melted
black pepper

Preheat oven to 450°F. Thaw fish, if frozen. Grease baking sheet and set aside. Rinse fish and pat dry. Cut into four serving-size pieces. Place buttermilk in a shallow dish. Place flour in another shallow dish. In a third shallow dish, mix bread crumbs, cheese, dill, butter, and a dash of black pepper.

Dip fish in milk, then in flour. Dip again in milk, then in bread crumb mixture, coating all sides thoroughly. Place prepared fish on baking sheet and bake uncovered for 8 minutes or until fish flakes easily with a fork.

Use Your Tool: Shallow glass dishes are versatile kitchen accessories—great for food preparation and serving.

Bearable Meal Suggestions: Beer and . . . Easy Cheesy Potato Bake (page 53) and Sesame Green Beans (page 50) or Green Bean Casserole (page 48).

GRILLED CHICKEN IN LIME CURRY SAUCE

Sounds impressive. Tastes impressive. Yet it's very simple to create. The key is in the marinade!

1/4 cup soy sauce
1/4 cup freshly squeezed lime juice
1 tablespoon minced garlic
1 tablespoon minced peeled ginger
1 1/2 teaspoons curry powder
4 skinless, boneless chicken breast halves
1 onion, sliced
1 cup chicken broth
salt and pepper

Whisk together soy, lime juice, garlic, ginger, and curry powder. Pour mixture into a large sealable plastic bag. Add chicken and onion. Seal bag well and refrigerate between 1 and 3 hours.

Prepare barbecue grill or oven broiler. Remove chicken from marinade. Strain marinade into medium saucepan and add broth. Boil sauce until it coats spoon, approximately 15 minutes. Meanwhile, grill or broil chicken until thoroughly cooked. Spoon sauce over chicken and serve.

Bearable Meal Suggestions: Beer and Sweet Pepper Salad (page 77).

UNCLE BEAU'S SUNDAY ROAST CHICKEN

1 roasting chicken (5 to 6 pounds)
1 lemon
kosher salt and freshly ground black pepper to taste
3 medium onions, quartered
3 cloves fresh garlic, peeled
2 bay leaves
fresh parsley, several sprigs
4 tablespoons melted butter
1 tablespoon dried thyme
1 tablespoon dried sage
1 tablespoon dried marjoram
8 carrots, cut in half
6 celery stalks with leaves, cut in half

Preheat oven to 475°F. Rinse chicken well inside and out under cold running water, and pat dry with paper towels. Make sure you remove the neck and giblet package from the cavity or your guests will find a nasty surprise when carving. Roll the lemon on the counter with the palm of your hand. Cut lemon in half and squeeze the juice over the skin of the chicken inside and out over a roasting pan. Liberally season the inside cavity and outside skin with salt and pepper. Put one half of the squeezed lemon, 2 onion quarters, garlic, bay leaves, and parsley inside the cavity of the chicken. Rub the outside of the chicken with an even coat of the melted butter. Mix together the thyme, sage, and marjoram, and crush the herbs in your hand as you sprinkle them evenly over the chicken.

Spread the carrots, celery, and remaining onion evenly in the bottom of the roasting pan. Place the chicken on top of the bed of vegetables, making sure it does not touch the bottom of the pan. Place the chicken in the preheated oven and roast at 475°F for 30 minutes. Reduce the temperature to 350°F and continue roasting until the juices from the thigh run clear, or the internal temperature of the thigh reaches 180°F (about 1 hour). If the skin looks like it might be getting too brown before the chicken is done, cover the breast and legs loosely with foil. Remove the chicken from the pan and let it rest at least 20 minutes before carving. Serve the roasted vegetables alongside the chicken.

SECTION VI:
BEYOND THE HONEYPOT

VERY BERRY RUBY COBBLER

Poor rhubarb—what a misunderstood root. This easy microwave dessert is a great way to discover just how delicious it can be.

3/4 cup sugar
3 tablespoons flour
1 (10-ounce) package frozen sweetened blackberries
1 (10-ounce) package frozen sweetened strawberries
3 cups rhubarb, cut into bite-size pieces

Topping

1/3 cup butter or margarine
1 cup rolled oats
1 cup unsifted all-purpose flour
3/4 cup brown sugar, firmly packed
1 teaspoon cinnamon
1/3 cup chopped nuts, optional

In a 3-quart microwave-safe baking dish, combine sugar and flour. Add frozen berries and cook uncovered in microwave oven on HIGH setting for 4 minutes, stirring once to mix berries. Stir in rhubarb and cook an additional 4 minutes on HIGH setting. Remove bowl from microwave.

Prepare topping by melting butter in a separate bowl for 30 seconds on HIGH setting. Remove from microwave. Stir in remaining ingredients into the melted butter. Spread topping evenly over fruit mixture. Cook on HIGH setting, uncovered, for 8 minutes or until mixture is bubbly toward center. For crispier topping, place under broiler for several minutes. Serve warm with whipped cream or ice cream.

Use Your Tool: If a 3-quart baking dish will not fit your microwave oven, divide mixture between two separate 2-quart dishes.

Bearable Meal Suggestions: Beer.

EASY PEACH BLUEBERRY COBBLER

Stanley: "I enjoy serving this year-round. Of course, it's better when fresh peaches are in season."

1/2 cup unsalted butter, melted
1 cup all-purpose flour
2 cups sugar
3 teaspoons baking powder
pinch of salt
1 cup milk
3 cups fresh peaches (3 to 4 medium peaches), peeled, pitted, and thinly sliced
1 cup fresh blueberries
1 tablespoon fresh lemon juice
several dashes of ground cinnamon
1/4 cup chopped pecans

Preheat oven to 375°F. Pour melted butter into a 13 x 9 x 2-inch baking dish.

In medium-sized bowl, combine flour, 1 cup of sugar, baking powder, and salt, and mix well. Stir in milk, mixing until just combined. Pour this batter over butter, but do not stir them together.

In a small saucepan, combine peaches, blueberries, lemon juice, and the remaining cup of sugar; bring to a boil over high heat, stirring constantly. Pour fruit mixture over the batter, but do not stir them together. Sprinkle with cinnamon and pecans. Bake in oven for 40 to 45 minutes or until top is golden brown. Serve warm or cold.

Use Your Tool: May substitute 2 cans of sliced, drained peaches for fresh if they are unavailable.

Bearable Meal Suggestions: Beer. Serve with Grandma's Homemade Ice Cream (page 119).

LONESTAR BROWNIES

This recipe proves the old saying, "Everything's BIGGER in Texas." These incredible brownies are not for the fainthearted—notice the 2 pounds of powdered sugar!

Cake Brownie

2 cups flour
2 cups sugar
1/2 cup butter
6 tablespoons baking cocoa
1 cup water
1/2 cup buttermilk
1 teaspoon baking soda
2 eggs, beaten
1 teaspoon vanilla

Preheat oven to 400°F. In a large bowl, sift together flour and sugar, and set aside.

In a large saucepan, melt butter. To that add cocoa and water, stirring until it comes to a boil. Pour over flour and sugar mixture. Add to bowl: buttermilk, baking soda, beaten eggs, and vanilla, blend until smooth. Pour into 13 x 18 x 1-inch greased and floured baking pan. Bake 15 to 20 minutes. Remove to cool.

Brownie Frosting

1 stick butter, melted
6 tablespoons baking cocoa
4 to 6 tablespoons milk
2 pounds powdered sugar
1 1/2 cups chopped walnuts
1 teaspoon vanilla

In a saucepan, combine butter, cocoa, and milk, and bring to a boil for 1 minute. Remove from heat and add powdered sugar, walnuts, and vanilla; mix until smooth. Spread on top of warm cake and let cool. Cut into large squares and serve.

Bearable Meal Suggestions: Beer. Serve with Grandma's Homemade Ice Cream (page 119).

BANANA PUDDING

Here is another classic layered dessert from our family archives. So many bananas, so little time!

3 (8-ounce) boxes vanilla or banana cream instant pudding mix
6 cups milk
1 (20-ounce) box vanilla wafers
8 large bananas, cut into half-inch slices
1 (16-ounce) container whipped topping

In a large mixing bowl, prepare boxes of instant pudding with milk, following box directions. In a 10 x 10 x 4-inch dish, layer vanilla wafers on bottom and place one row along bottom sides. Place slices of two bananas over wafers, followed by 1/3 of the pudding mixture. Continue this order of layering ingredients 2 more times until you reach the top of the dish. Cover and refrigerate, preferably for 1 hour. Top each serving with whipped topping.

Use Your Tool: To avoid lumps in your instant pudding, use a hand mixer.

Bearable Meal Suggestions: Beer or a tall glass of cold milk.

BEAR IN THE WOODS

The great taste of this dessert is no reflection on its name. However, once you see it served in a bowl, we think you'll understand.

1 3/4 cups flour
3/4 cup butter, room temperature
1 (8-ounce) package cream cheese
1 cup powdered sugar
2 cups whipped topping
2 (8-ounce) boxes chocolate instant pudding mix
3 cups milk
1 cup chopped nuts

Preheat oven to 350°F. In a 9 x 13-inch baking pan, blend flour and butter and pat mixture into the bottom of pan. Bake for 12 to 15 minutes. Remove from oven and cool completely.

In a mixing bowl, blend cream cheese, powdered sugar, and 1/2 cup of whipped topping, and spread over cooled flour crust. In another bowl, prepare the instant pudding and milk and spread over cream cheese mixture. Top with remaining whipped topping and sprinkle with nuts. Refrigerate overnight.

Use Your Tool: Hint—a kitchen mixer is your friend.

Bearable Meal Suggestions: Beer or a tall, cold glass of milk.

CREAM PUFFS

A dessert filled with a creamy center in *this* book? We could explain the relevance, but why?

Puffs

1 cup water
1/2 cup butter
1 cup flour, sifted
4 eggs

Filling

1 cup sugar
1/3 cup + 1 tablespoon flour
dash of salt
3 egg yolks
2 eggs
3 cups milk
2 teaspoons vanilla extract

Puff Directions: Preheat oven to 400°F. In a medium saucepan, bring water and butter to a boil. Stir in sifted flour. Beat eggs into mixture one at a time. Remove from heat. Distribute mixture in a nonstick cream puff baking pan and bake for 45 to 50 minutes. Cut baked puffs in half, add filling mixture, and replace top of puff.

Filling Directions: Place all ingredients into a medium saucepan and bring to a boil. Reduce heat and cook until mixture coats the back of a wooden spoon. Remove from heat and let cool. Filling should have a pudding consistency. Puffs may be filled when warm or refrigerated.

Use Your Tool: Make these once and you will always be grateful to have a cream puff pan in your kitchen.

Bearable Meal Suggestions: Beer. Serve after a hearty meal of Mom's Meat Loaf (page 90).

CHOCOLATE LOAF

"If you're worried about cholesterol or heart disease, this is NOT the recipe for you!" Stanley admits. "I agree," PJ adds. "I needed a defibrillator after eating this amazing slice of heaven! Your life will never be the same again!"

18 ounces semisweet chocolate
1 3/4 cups unsalted butter (3 1/2 sticks)
10 eggs, separated
fresh raspberries (garnish)

Line a 12 1/2 x 4 1/2-inch loaf pan with enough aluminum foil to hang over sides of pan approximately 3 inches. Place chocolate and butter in a large microwave-safe bowl and cook on HIGH setting for about 5 minutes or until all ingredients are melted. Make sure to blend chocolate and butter until smooth. In a separate bowl, add egg yolks and 1 cup of the melted chocolate/butter mixture and whisk until smooth. This will temper the eggs so they won't scramble. Then add the remaining chocolate/butter mixture and whisk thoroughly. In a separate bowl or in a mixer, whisk egg whites until soft peaks form. Gently fold egg whites into chocolate mixture in three portions. Pour combined mixture into prepared loaf pan. Tap pan on a hard surface to remove air bubbles. Smooth over top with spatula. Chill at least 8 hours or overnight in refrigerator. To serve, invert loaf pan onto serving platter and remove pan and aluminum foil. Garnish with fresh raspberries.

Raspberry Sauce

1 (10-ounce) bag frozen raspberries, thawed
1/2 cup sugar

Combine ingredients in a food processor and blend until smooth. Strain through a fine sieve in order to remove seeds. Coat serving plates with raspberry sauce and top with a slice of the chocolate loaf.

Use Your Tool: The loaf will slice most easily with a long thin knife that has been dipped in hot water.

Bearable Meal Suggestions: Beer.

No Bear Kitchen
Is Complete Without . . .

COOL WHIP

It's hard to imagine what a Bear's kitchen (or bedroom) was like before 1967—the year Kraft Foods introduced Cool Whip as the first prewhipped topping. According to <www.kraftfoods.com>, "across America six tubs of Cool Whip are purchased every second."

We're guessing that more than a few hungry Bears have something to do with this statistic.

CARROT ZUCCHINI CAKE

Not in the habit of eating your vegetables? Try them for dessert instead.

4 eggs
2 cups sugar
2 1/2 cups all-purpose flour
2 teaspoons baking soda
2 teaspoons baking powder
2 teaspoons ground cinnamon
1 teaspoon ground cloves
1 teaspoon ground allspice
1 teaspoon ground ginger
1/2 teaspoon nutmeg
1 teaspoon salt
1 1/3 cups vegetable oil
2 cups finely shredded carrots
2 cups finely shredded zucchini
1 cup coarsely chopped pecans

Preheat oven to 350°F. Grease three 9-inch round baking pans. In a large mixing bowl, beat eggs and sugar until smooth. In a separate bowl combine all dry ingredients. Gradually beat in oil. Add dry ingredients to egg mixture and beat 4 minutes. Stir in carrots, zucchini, and pecans. Blend until all ingredients are well combined. Pour mixture evenly into baking pans and bake for 30 to 35 minutes or until top springs back when lightly touched. Cool 5 minutes before removing from pans. Once removed, cool completely on wire rack.

Frosting

1 (8-ounce) package cream cheese, softened
1/2 cup butter, softened (1 stick)
5 cups powdered sugar
2 teaspoons vanilla
chopped pecans (as garnish)

In a large bowl, beat cream cheese and butter until smooth. Add sugar and vanilla and continue beating until sugar is dissolved. Spread frosting between cake layers and over top and sides. Garnish with chopped nuts.

MOM'S OATMEAL PIE

This dessert is utterly Bear worthy—it's easy, delicious, and so very comforting! See for yourself.

2 eggs, slightly beaten
3/4 cup maple syrup
1/2 cup sugar
1/2 cup packed brown sugar
1/2 cup milk
1/2 cup butter, melted
1 teaspoon vanilla
1 cup flaked coconut
3/4 cup rolled oats
1/2 cup walnuts or pecans, chopped
1 (9-inch) unbaked piecrust
whipped topping

Preheat oven to 375°F. In a large mixing bowl, combine eggs, maple syrup, sugar, brown sugar, milk, butter, and vanilla. Stir well. Add coconut, rolled oats, and nuts, and blend completely. Pour into unbaked piecrust. Bake for 35 to 40 minutes or until a knife inserted into center of pie comes away clean. Cool on wire rack. Serve with whipped topping. Refrigerate within 2 hours.

Use Your Tool: In our opinion, ready-made piecrusts are a great food invention—use them.

Bearable Meal Suggestions: Beer. Great idea for holiday dessert planning!

NANNIE'S PECAN PIE

PJ: "This is a great Southern recipe from one of the greatest women in my life—my Aunt Anne. I love you, Nannie."

1/4 cup butter, softened
1/2 cup brown sugar
3 eggs
1/2 cup maple syrup
1 teaspoon vanilla
1/2 teaspoon salt
1 1/2 cups pecan pieces
1 (9-inch) unbaked piecrust

    Preheat oven to 450°F. In a large bowl, mix butter and brown sugar until creamy. Beat in eggs—one at a time. To this mixture, stir in maple syrup, vanilla, salt, and pecan pieces. Blend until smooth.
    Pour mixture into piecrust and place into oven. Reduce heat to 350°F and bake for 40 minutes or until a fork inserted comes away clean.

Bearable Meal Suggestions: Beer. Serve after a great Southern meal of barbecued chicken and Deep South Potato Salad (page 40).

DADDY'S FAVORITE PEACH PIE

"Another summer favorite that I enjoyed growing up—thanks, Mom!" Sincerely, Stanley.

Piecrust

1 cup oatmeal
1/2 cup slivered almonds
1/2 cup brown sugar
1/3 cup butter, softened

Preheat oven to 350°F. In a mixing bowl, combine all ingredients well. Pour into 9-inch pie pan. Form crust by pressing mixture onto bottom and sides of pan. Place pie pan in oven for 5 minutes. Remove and cool.

Filling

1 (3-ounce) package orange JELL-O Brand Gelatin Dessert
1 cup hot water
3 to 4 cups sliced fresh peaches
1 pint vanilla ice cream, softened

In a large bowl, mix JELL-O and hot water until dissolved. Add peaches and softened ice cream and stir until well blended. Pour mixture into baked pie shell and chill 3 to 4 hours.

Bearable Meal Suggestions: Beer. Ideally served with summer season favorites.

BANANA SPLIT CAKE

Oh, the things we can do with bananas!

2 cups graham cracker crumbs
1 1/2 cups butter, melted
2 cups powdered sugar
2 eggs
4 bananas, sliced
1 (14-ounce) can crushed pineapple, drained
1 container whipped topping
1/2 cup chopped walnuts

In a large bowl, combine graham cracker crumbs and 1/2 cup melted butter. Mix well and pour into bottom of a 13 x 9 x 3-inch baking pan. In a separate bowl, combine powdered sugar, eggs, and remaining butter. Beat 15 minutes in an electric mixer. Spread over crumb mixture in pan. Layer sliced bananas, then top with pineapple. Add whipped topping and smooth with spatula. Sprinkle with nuts. Refrigerate 12 to 24 hours.

Use Your Tool: If you're going to beat anything for 15 minutes, you should use an electric mixer.

Bearable Meal Suggestions: Beer.

OVER-THE-TOP EASY BAKE

This is white trash cooking at its best and only served at the finest of trailer park barbecues . . . until now.

1 box devil's food cake mix
1 (14-ounce) can sweetened condensed milk
1 (8-ounce) jar caramel sauce
1 (8-ounce) jar chocolate fudge sauce
1 container whipped topping
1 English toffee candy bar, coarsely chopped

Prepare cake mix per box instructions using a 9 x 12-inch pan. Bake and let cool.

Once cake has cooled completely, poke holes into cake every 1 1/2 inches, using the handle of a wooden spoon. Pour sweetened condensed milk over top of cake and let soak. Pour caramel sauce over cake, followed by chocolate fudge sauce. Spread whipped topping over top and sprinkle with chopped toffee bar. Cover with plastic wrap and refrigerate for 24 hours.

Bearable Meal Suggestions: Beer . . . with an insulin chaser.

OUR FAVORITE NEW YORK-STYLE CHEESECAKE

We couldn't resist adding this one to the book—woof!

1 pound ricotta cheese
2 (8-ounce packages) cream cheese, softened
4 eggs
1 1/2 cup sugar
1 teaspoon lemon juice
1 teaspoon vanilla
3 tablespoons cornstarch
3 tablespoons flour
1/4 cup butter, melted
1 pint sour cream

Preheat oven to 325°F. In a food processor, blend ricotta cheese, cream cheese, and eggs until smooth. Add all other ingredients and blend until very smooth. Pour into a greased 10-inch springform pan. Bake for one hour. DO NOT OPEN OVEN. After cooking 1 hour, increase oven temperature to 375°F. Bake for an additional 10 minutes. Turn oven off and let cake rest in oven for 30 to 40 minutes. Remove from oven and LET COOL COMPLETELY in springform pan. Upon cooling, remove sides of pan and chill at least 3 to 5 hours prior to serving.

Use Your Tool: A springform pan is an absolute necessity for this recipe—and a worthy addition to your kitchenware.

Bearable Meal Suggestions: Beer.

EASY BLUEBERRY CHEESECAKE

3 cups graham cracker crumbs
3/4 cup butter, melted
2 (8-ounce) packages cream cheese
1 cup sugar
1 container whipped topping
2 bananas, sliced
1 can blueberry pie filling

Preheat oven to 350°F. In a large bowl, combine graham cracker crumbs and melted butter. Mix well and pour into bottom of an 11 x 14-inch baking pan. Press mixture into bottom of pan. Bake for 3 to 5 minutes (allows crust to be cut easier when serving). Remove from oven and cool.

In a mixing bowl, combine cream cheese and sugar, and beat until smooth. Add whipped topping, blend thoroughly, and set aside. Place sliced bananas on top of graham cracker crust. Pour cream cheese filling over top and chill 3 to 4 hours. Once chilled, top with blueberry pie filling.

Bearable Meal Suggestions: Beer. Great for potlucks!

CHOCOLATE PUDDING CAKE

The magic of this recipe is in the way the chocolate cake and pudding "flip" when baked. It's a beautiful thing.

2 ounces unsweetened chocolate, chopped
1/2 cup unsalted butter, softened
1 1/2 cups sugar
1 cup all-purpose flour, sifted
1 1/2 teaspoons baking powder
1/2 teaspoon salt
1/2 cup milk
2 teaspoons vanilla
1/2 cup brown sugar, firmly packed
3 rounded tablespoons unsweetened cocoa
1 1/2 cups boiling water

Preheat oven to 350°F. Grease a 9-inch square baking pan. Place chocolate in a small microwave-safe bowl and cook on a HIGH setting until chocolate is melted and smooth. Let cool slightly. In a separate bowl, combine butter and 3/4 cup of sugar. Using a whisk or electric mixer, beat until light and fluffy. Sift together flour, baking powder, and salt onto the butter mixture; then add milk. Stir with whisk or mixer on a low speed until well mixed. Fold in melted chocolate and one teaspoon of vanilla. Spread mixture evenly into prepared pan.

In the same bowl, stir together remaining sugar, brown sugar, and cocoa. Sprinkle this over the batter in the pan. Add remaining 1 teaspoon of vanilla into boiling water and slowly pour water over the batter—so as not to disturb it much. Bake until firm, approximately 1 hour. Let cool slightly.

To serve, cut into squares. Spoon some of the sauce from the bottom of pan over each serving.

Use Your Tool: Once again, it's easier to combine ingredients with an electric mixer if you have one.

Bearable Meal Suggestions: Beer. Serve any time you need a "chocolate fix."

GRANDMA'S HOMEMADE ICE CREAM

"I remember my siblings and I struggling to make this, using an old-fashioned ice cream churn and rock salt," Stanley recalls. "Now you can get the same results in half the time by using electric ice cream makers."

1 1/2 cups milk, scalded
3/4 cup sugar
3 eggs, slightly beaten
1 teaspoon salt
1 tablespoon vanilla
3 cups heavy cream

In a saucepan, blend all ingredients and cook over medium heat until slightly thick (clings to spoon). Remove from heat and cool. Pour into ice cream maker and follow appropriate directions per machine.

Use Your Tool: You can still apply this recipe to an old-fashioned crank mixer. However, electric ice cream makers are much easier.

Bearable Meal Suggestions: Beer. This ice cream complements any of our other desserts.

Recipe Index

Apple-Nut Cinnamon Rolls, 31
Auntie's Dill Dip, 8

Banana Bread, 35
Banana Pudding, 104
Banana Split Cake, 114
Bear Belly Bombers, 12
Bear Daddy's Baked Beans, 46
Bear in the Woods, 105
Bear-to-Go Sandwich, 27
Beef Fajitas, 89
Beef Stroganoff, 67
Big Banana Shake, 14
Blueberry Orange Muffins, 34
Brat Bake, 79

Cabin Fever Soup, 54
Carrot Zucchini Cake, 109
Cheese on Rye Pizzas, 9
Cheesy Chicken Casserole, 61
Chicken Fajitas, 89
Chili-and-Chip Dip, 15
Chinese Chicken Salad, 74
Chocolate Loaf, 107
Chocolate Pudding Cake, 118
Cookie Brittle, 16
Corn Fritters, 51
Corn Potato Frittata, 29
Cornmeal Dressin', 45
Cream Puffs, 106
Creole Beans and Sausage, 66
Cub Salad, 76
Curry Chicken Salad, 75

Daddy's Favorite Peach Pie, 113
Deep South Potato Salad, 40

Dinner Party Pork Chops, 94
Dutch Apple Pancakes, 22

Easy Blueberry Cheesecake, 117
Easy Cheesy Potato Bake, 53
Easy Peach Blueberry Cobbler, 102

Fiery Chicken Enchiladas, 69
Flamin' Flank Steak, 86
Fruity Barbecue Wings, 17
Fur-ocious Pot Roast, 85

Garlic Chicken Stroganoff, 68
Grandma's Barbecue Beef, 84
Grandma's Homemade Ice Cream, 119
Green Bean Casserole, 48
Grilled Chicken in Lime Curry Sauce, 96

Hobo Hash, 21
Hot German Potato Salad, 41
Husbear Burgers, 83

Johnny Bear-Zetti, 62

Lonestar Brownies, 103

Manly, Yes—Macaroni Salad, 58
Microwave Popcorn, 10
Mini Franks, 11
Mom's Meat Loaf, 90
Mom's Oatmeal Pie, 110

Nannie's Pecan Pie, 111

Onion Ring Beer Batter, 7
Our Favorite New York-Style
    Cheesecake, 116
Overnight Rolls, 33
Over-the-Top Easy Bake, 115

Peach Canyon Quesadillas, 18
Pizza Burgers, 13
Polar Bear Chili, 73
Popovers, 28
Pork Steaks, 92
Port Stuffing, 44
Potato and Onion Casserole, 43
Potatoes Chantal, 57

Raunchy Ranch Munch, 6
Real Bears Eat Quiche, 30
Russian River Oven-Baked Fish, 95

Sausage Gravy and Biscuits, 25
Sesame Green Beans, 50
Slow-Simmered Country Ribs, 93

Spaghetti Carbonara, 63
(Squeal Like a) Piggy Mac, 64
Sweet Hot Chili, 72
Sweet Kibble, 5
Sweet Pepper Salad, 77
Sweety Potatoes Anna, 42

(Touch My) Monkey Bread, 32
Tuna Rice Skillet, 71

Uncle Beau's Standing Rib (Big Meat),
    88
Uncle Beau's Sunday Roast Chicken,
    97

Very Berry Ruby Cobbler, 101

What-a-Crock-Pot Stew, 78
What's It All About ... Alfredo, 55
Woofy Breakfast Stew, 24

Yankee Potato Salad, 39

Subject Index

Alfredo, 55
Apples
    Apple-Nut Cinnamon Rolls, 31
    Dutch Apple Pancakes, 22

Bananas
    Banana Bread, 35
    Banana Pudding, 104
    Banana Split Cake, 114
    Big Banana Shake, 14
Beans
    Bear Daddy's Baked Beans, 46
    Creole Beans and Sausage, 66
    Green Bean Casserole, 48
    Sesame Green Beans, 50
Beef, 91
    Beef Fajitas, 89
    Beef Stroganoff, 67
    Flamin' Flank Steak, 86
    Fur-ocious Pot Roast, 85
    Grandma's Barbecue Beef, 84
    Husbear Burgers, 83
    Mom's Meat Loaf, 90
    Pizza Burgers, 13
    Uncle Beau's Standing Rib (Big
      Meat), 88
    What-a-Crock Pot Stew, 78
Beer, onion ring batter, 7
Biscuits, sausage gravy and, 25
Bisquick, 26
Blueberries
    Blueberry Orange Muffins, 34
    Easy Blueberry Cheesecake, 117
    Easy Peach Blueberry Cobbler, 102
Bratwurst, 79
Breads/rolls/muffins
    Apple-Nut Cinnamon Rolls, 31
    Banana Bread, 35
    Blueberry Orange Muffins, 34
    Overnight Rolls, 33
    (Touch My) Monkey Bread, 32

Breakfast
    Apple-Nut Cinnamon Rolls, 31
    Banana Bread, 35
    Bear-to-Go Sandwich, 27
    Blueberry Orange Muffins, 34
    Corn Potato Frittata, 29
    Dutch Apple Pancakes, 22
    Hobo Hash, 21
    Overnight Rolls, 33
    Popovers, 28
    Real Bears Eat Quiche, 30
    Sausage Gravy and Biscuits, 25
    (Touch My) Monkey Bread, 32
    Woofy Breakfast Stew, 24
Brownies, 103
Burgers/sandwiches
    Bear-to-Go Sandwich, 27
    Husbear Burgers, 83
    Pizza Burgers, 13
Butter, strawberry, 28

Cakes/pies
    Banana Split Cake, 114
    Carrot Zucchini Cake, 109
    Chocolate Pudding Cake, 118
    Daddy's Favorite Peach Pie, 113
    Easy Blueberry Cheesecake, 117
    Mom's Oatmeal Pie, 110
    Nannie's Pecan Pie, 111
    Our Favorite New York-Style
      Cheesecake, 116
    Over-the-Top Easy Bake, 115
Chicken
    Cheesy Chicken Casserole, 61
    Chicken Fajitas, 89
    Chinese Chicken Salad, 74
    Cub Salad, 76
    Curry Chicken Salad, 75
    Fiery Chicken Enchiladas, 69
    Fruity Barbecue Wings, 17

Chicken *(continued)*
   Garlic Chicken Stroganoff, 68
   Grilled Chicken in Lime Curry
      Sauce, 96
   Uncle Beau's Sunday Roast
      Chicken, 97
Chili
   Chili-and-Chip Dip, 15
   Polar Bear Chili, 73
   Sweet Hot Chili, 72
Cobbler
   Easy Peach Blueberry Cobbler, 102
   Very Berry Ruby Cobbler, 101
Cookies, 16
Cool Whip, 108
Corn
   Corn Fritters, 51
   Corn Potato Frittata, 51
Cornflakes, 52
Cream of mushroom soup, 70

Desserts
   Banana Pudding, 104
   Banana Split Cake, 114
   Bear in the Woods, 105
   Carrot Zucchini Cake, 109
   Chocolate Loaf, 107
   Chocolate Pudding Cake, 118
   Cream Puffs, 106
   Daddy's Favorite Peach Pie, 113
   Easy Blueberry Cheesecake, 117
   Easy Peach Blueberry Cobbler, 102
   Grandma's Homemade Ice Cream,
      119
   Lonestar Brownies, 103
   Mom's Oatmeal Pie, 110
   Nannie's Pecan Pie, 111
   Over-the-Top Easy Bake, 115
   Our Favorite New York-Style
      Cheesecake, 116
   Very Berry Ruby Cobbler, 101
Dips
   Auntie's Dill Dip, 8
   Chili-and-Chip Dip, 15
Dressing, cornmeal, 45

Enchiladas, 69
Entrées
   Beef Stroganoff, 67
   Brat Bake, 79
   Cheesy Chicken Casserole, 61
   Chinese Chicken Salad, 74
   Creole Beans and Sausage, 66
   Cub Salad, 76
   Curry Chicken Salad, 75
   Fiery Chicken Enchiladas, 69
   Garlic Chicken Stroganoff, 68
   Johnny Bear-Zetti, 62
   Polar Bear Chili, 73
   Spaghetti Carbonara, 63
   (Squeal Like a) Piggy Mac, 64
   Sweet Hot Chili, 72
   Sweet Pepper Salad, 77
   Tuna Rice Skillet, 71
   What-a-Crock-Pot Stew, 78

Fish
   Russian River Oven-Baked Fish, 95
   Tuna Rice Skillet, 71
Frittata, corn potato, 29

Ground beef, 91

Ice cream, 119

Muffins/breads/rolls
   Apple-Nut Cinnamon Rolls, 31
   Banana Bread, 35
   Blueberry Orange Muffins, 34
   Overnight Rolls, 33
   (Touch My) Monkey Bread, 32

Onion
   Onion Ring Beer Batter, 7
   Potato and Onion Casserole, 43

Pancakes, 22
Pasta
  Cub Salad, 76
  Johnny Bear-Zetti, 62
  Manly, Yes—Macaroni Salad, 58
  Spaghetti Carbonara, 63
  (Squeal Like a) Piggy Mac, 64
  Sweet Pepper Salad, 77
Peaches
  Daddy's Favorite Peach Pie, 113
  Easy Peach Blueberry Cobbler, 102
  Peach Canyon Quesadillas, 18
Pies/cakes
  Banana Split Cake, 114
  Carrot Zucchini Cake, 109
  Chocolate Pudding Cake, 118
  Daddy's Favorite Peach Pie, 113
  Easy Blueberry Cheesecake, 117
  Mom's Oatmeal Pie, 110
  Nannie's Pecan Pie, 111
  Our Favorite New York-Style
      Cheesecake, 116
  Over-the-Top Easy Bake, 115
Pizza
  Cheese on Rye Pizzas, 9
  Pizza Burgers, 13
Popcorn, 10
Popovers, 28
Pork
  Dinner Party Pork Chops, 94
  Pork Steaks, 92
  Pork Stuffing, 44
  Slow-Simmered Country Ribs, 93
Potatoes
  Corn Potato Frittata, 29
  Deep South Potato Salad, 40
  Easy Cheesy Potato Bake, 53
  Hobo Hash, 21
  Hot German Potato Salad, 41
  Potato and Onion Casserole, 43
  Potatoes Chantal, 57
  Sweety Potatoes Anna, 42
  Yankee Potato Salad, 39
Pudding
  Banana Pudding, 104
  Bear in the Woods, 105

Quesadillas, 18
Quiche, 30

Rice, 71
Rolls/muffins/breads
  Apple-Nut Cinnamon Rolls, 31
  Banana Bread, 35
  Blueberry Orange Muffins, 34
  Overnight Rolls, 33
  (Touch My) Monkey Bread, 32

Salads
  Chinese Chicken Salad, 74
  Cub Salad, 76
  Curry Chicken Salad, 75
  Deep South Potato Salad, 40
  Hot German Potato Salad, 41
  Manly, Yes—Macaroni Salad, 58
  Sweet Pepper Salad, 77
  Yankee Potato Salad, 39
Sandwiches/burgers
  Bear-to-Go Sandwich, 27
  Husbear Burgers, 83
  Pizza Burgers, 13
Side dishes
  Bear Daddy's Baked Beans, 46
  Cabin Fever Soup, 54
  Corn Fritters, 51
  Cornmeal Dressin', 45
  Deep South Potato Salad, 40
  Easy Cheesy Potato Bake, 53
  Green Bean Casserole, 48
  Hot German Potato Salad, 41
  Manly, Yes—Macaroni Salad, 58
  Pork Stuffing, 44
  Potato and Onion Casserole, 43
  Potatoes Chantal, 57
  Sesame Green Beans, 50
  Sweety Potatoes Anna, 42
  What's It All About ... Alfredo, 55
  Yankee Potato Salad, 39
Snacks
  Auntie's Dill Dip, 8
  Bear Belly Bombers, 12
  Big Banana Shake, 14
  Cheese on Rye Pizzas, 9
  Chili-and-Chip Dip, 15
  Cookie Brittle, 16
  Fruity Barbecue Wings, 17
  Microwave Popcorn, 10
  Mini Franks, 11

Snacks *(continued)*
    Onion Ring Beer Batter, 7
    Peach Canyon Quesadillas, 18
    Pizza Burgers, 13
    Raunchy Ranch Munch, 6
    Sweet Kibble, 5
Soups/stews
    Cabin Fever Soup, 54
    What-a-Crock Pot Stew, 78
    Woofy Breakfast Stew, 24
Strawberry butter, 28
Stuffing, pork, 44

Velveeta, 47